Fun
WITHOUT
Dick and Jane

YOUR GUIDE TO A DELIGHTFULLY EMPTY NEST

Happy next step!

by Christie Mellor

CHRONICLE BOOKS

SAN FRANCISCO

D1009910

With love to my witty, intelligent, and always supportive nest-mate, Richard, who brings me peonies, music, hilarity, and a lot of really great titles.

Text copyright © 2012 by Christie Mellor.
Illustrations copyright © 2012 by Christie Mellor.

All rights reserved. No part of this book may be reproduced in any form without written permission from the publisher.

Library of Congress Cataloging-in-Publication Data available.

ISBN 978-1-4521-0597-0

Manufactured in China

Design by Tracy Johnson

10 9 8 7 6 5 4 3 2 1

Chronicle Books LLC
680 Second Street
San Francisco, California 94107

www.chroniclebooks.com

TABLE OF CONTENTS

INTRODUCTION

And a Child Shall Leave Them

SHE'S LEAVING HOME. BUH-BYE!

You had a farewell party (or two), took her on a couple of shopping sprees, and looked over her shoulder as she registered for classes online and became acquainted with her new dorm mate through Facebook. You wondered aloud whether said dorm mate didn't maybe look "like someone who smokes a lot of pot." You helped her pack, making sure she had extra washcloths and those furry socks she likes to wear to bed.

Now she's gone. She really left. And you're already wondering when the first Parents' Visiting Day will be. Soon, you hope.

Perhaps you haven't gone so far as to rent an apartment within spitting distance of your child's dorm room. But you *do* check her Facebook page first thing every morning, leaving little notes on her "wall," sending her long messages throughout the day. And it's so great that she taught you how to text, because now you can check in constantly at the touch of a thumb, just to ask her how things are going. You know the details of lost books and missed classes, and who's hooking up with whom on her dorm floor. You're finding the house a little quiet, so you spend your days organizing her old high school papers and projects, finally getting around to selecting the really standout pieces of elementary school art and sending them out for framing. You mail her a weekly care package full of her favorite snacks, just in case she's feeling a little peckish between meals. And when your child complains about a professor being a "really hard grader," well, you just call up that professor and give him a piece of your mind.

If you find yourself inching toward this kind of insanity in the wake of your child leaving the nest, it could be time to assess your own life. Have you spent the last eighteen years devoting every waking moment to your child's survival, happiness, enrichment, and entertainment? Have you come to the realization that your child has been your only hobby? Do you feel like your only reason for existence is gone, leaving you with nothing to do but create scrapbooks of your child's first eighteen years of life?

"But," you say, "what else is there to do other than create scrapbooks of my child's first eighteen years of life? And what if we really like each other and *want* to talk on the phone five times a day? You, Christie Mellor, are a bad, bad mother, who must hate her child."

That is not completely true. I only hate him when he does that annoying thing with his hair and when he disagrees with me over his excessive use of the computer.

Look—you are not abandoning your child. And *he* is not abandoning *you*. Your child is entering the first stage of his life as an adult. That's a *good* thing. Getting away from his childhood home is an important step in his growth and maturity. And—who could've imagined?—in yours.

Here's the thing: Kids grow up. They leave home. They're supposed to do that. Now it's time to rekindle some former interests, talents, skills, and dreams. It's time to find something else to do. Finding something else to focus on doesn't mean you don't love your children. It doesn't mean you have ceased to be a mother. It doesn't mean you aren't interested in their lives. But now your relationship with your kids will ebb and flow, and it's a perfect opportunity to explore those passions you left behind when you became a parent. At the very least, you're probably going to need a few activities to fill up those extra hours you've got.

This handy guide aims to get you through that initial empty-nest adjustment period—and beyond. Because the "beyond" part is really important: Wouldn't it be nice to be well into living your own life by the time your little darling has graduated from college?

Sure, "living your own life" is probably something you should have been doing all along, even with youngsters at home. One hopes that we've managed to pursue interests and hobbies other than our children while simultaneously being a parent. But if you find that your "other" life somehow dropped by the wayside while you were busy creating the perfect child, perhaps you can pick up where you left off. Now that that perfect child has left home, it's time to create your perfect life.

part 1

So Long, Farewell

Big Mom on Campus

YOU HELPED HIM WITH HIS KINDERGARTEN ALPHABET HOMEWORK. You've seen him through Mommy and Me; Gymboree; endless weekends of T-ball, Little League, ballet, and piano lessons; and a plethora of playdates. You hired that high-end math tutor in third grade and helped him build that relief map (with a working volcano!) in fourth grade—because, after all, you both wanted it to be "perfect." You made sure he always had the best teachers, even if it meant the principal of the school ducked into a doorway every time she saw you coming. You helped your child find service and volunteering opportunities starting in sixth grade—because really, it's never too soon to start thinking about what looks good on a college application. You're betting that there won't be many kids who built shelters for the homeless *and* worked as a medical aide in Guatemala during spring break. And yes, as far as you're concerned, manning the Water-Dunk Booth at the school fair does count as "community service."

You got through high school together, as a team. The AP classes and academic workload piled up, but you knuckled down, along with your child. Sure, you started to freak out during sophomore year, what with college looming on the horizon. It didn't seem too early to start panicking—you've been attending College Night with your child since eighth grade!—but by the tenth grade, it was starting to seem like a *real* reality.

Junior year was a blur of precollege activity. Three hundred dollars an hour for an SAT coach seemed a little steep, but everyone else was doing it, and you didn't want to be behind the curve. You pored over college brochures and searched campuses online, but so many moms and dads seemed to be taking their children on grand College Tours that you planned an elaborate fifteen-stop tour as well. Sure, it meant no vacations for the next few years. But your little darling was worth it.

And you were pretty darn proud of those college essays: concise, thoughtful, and with just that bright edge of humor. (I mean, of course your child *wrote* them, but you had to help a little with the outline. And the basic concept. And he really needed a hand with that introduction. But he *wrote* the essay himself. Once you got that first draft started. And did the editing.) You were thrilled when all your hard work paid off and the college acceptance letters started arriving.

Okay, fine, maybe there were a few rejections. But must we dwell on that kind of negativity? It's important to remember, he probably hasn't had to deal with much rejection in his life yet (barring an occasional kickball pick, or a painful crush or two), from his days in Little League, when everyone got a trophy simply for showing up, to his school career, throughout which he was told he was wonderful in every way. You've fought on his behalf when you felt he was unfairly graded, and you did what you could to help ease the unpleasantness when a few of his teachers did not appreciate his gifts as much as they might have. Now, apparently, a few Ivy League colleges don't recognize the value of his well-rounded, creative approach to learning. Perhaps his hopes of a Harvard or Princeton education have been quashed; but since they were really more your hopes than his, he's actually fine with it. Whew!

Luckily, he made it into a decent college, and you got busy buying him dorm furniture and supplies. The days became a whirl of preparation, a series of precious snapshots, of fleeting moments: your child, taking finals. Ordering his cap and gown. Signing his yearbook. Vomiting up the vodka smuggled in by the valedictorian on prom night.

And now it's College Move-in Day! You drove hundreds of miles with a packed car and a small U-Haul trailer. After all, how can he do without a microwave oven in his dorm, for late-night snacks? And of course the large flat-screen TV that he'll need for his PlayStation 2 and movies? The desktop computer and printer (plus his laptop for classes) are a must, as is his new iPad. As well as the steamer trunk full of bath towels, bedding, and his special hypoallergenic mattress pad.

Move-in Day! *Day?* You've decided to stay for the *week*. Just to get your youngster settled. In fact . . . what a nice location! Maybe it *would* be a good idea to get a little apartment nearby, just to help your child get acclimated to college life.

Just about now you should be hearing the sound of a large vehicle coming to a screeching halt. Okay, you weren't really thinking of moving down the street from your child's dorm, were you? Parents: It's not his first day of preschool. Your eighteen-year-old *will be okay* if he's living in a dorm that's more than a hundred or a thousand miles away from you.

If four or five days have gone by since you arrived to "settle" your child into his dorm . . . if you find yourself wanting to stay on just a few more days, or if you find yourself standing in front of the postings in the window of the local real estate office and you don't really know how you got there . . . if you find yourself wanting to hang out in your child's dorm room "just one more night," or you start Friending your child's new dorm mates . . . then it's time to extricate yourself. Just be honest with yourself. You are not alone, you know: It's now common to find actual seminars offered by the college for parents, to help you face the moment of departure. The seminars came about because of the sheer numbers of parents who simply would not leave their child on move-in day. If this sounds appealing to you, then sign up immediately. Or, just take a deep breath. Say your good-byes, get in your car, and drive away.

Now, just to be clear: I'm not suggesting you coldly send your child far, far away, change the locks on your door, and never look back. You may have a very close relationship with your child. I will be the first to admit, as a mother of boys, that my relationship with my boys may not be the same as yours with your girls. As sweet and sensitive and caring as my college boy may be, he is not likely to call me five times a day to gush over the cute girl in Economics or opine about the relative awesomeness of his Comparative Lit professor. Nor is he apt to text me about love, music, and adorable boots. Okay, sometimes about music. But never about footwear.

I have friends who are as inseparable from their daughters as Siamese twins. They chat with each other ten times a day, and when the daughters come home for visits, they shop, giggle, and endlessly share. I admit I sometimes wistfully long for a little more sharing than a Facebook message reminding me to fill out the financial-aid applications and telling me, "Everything's going great! ☺" And it's true I get more information from a glance at my son's Facebook profile than anything he's ever written in an e-mail or told me in a phone call. But once in a while, when I do see him in person and we're on a walk or sitting together over a cup of something, we do end up talking. And he does fill in the gaps, and clue me in on details. He just does it in his own way. Sadly, there is no shopping involved.

So, every parent has their own unique relationship with their child, and I'm not here to tell you that you shouldn't enjoy a close, warm, and loving friendship with your kids after they move away. That kind of connection is more rare than it should be among parents and children, and is to be cherished and applauded. I'm simply suggesting that part of the experience of leaving home is, your child gets to discover *who he is*—without his parents!—just as part of having your children leave home is about you discovering who you are without your children to define you. Of course you'll always be a mother, and they'll always be your babies. Being a mother may define who you are forever, and you may want it that way. But you can define yourself in other ways, too. And as the kids leave the nest (as they mostly tend to do), you're going to find yourself with plenty of extra time on your hands for finding new ways to define yourself.

It's time to say good-bye. And how in the world do you do that? Well, if acceptance is not exactly coming naturally to you, the answer may lie more in what *not* to do. If you've been asking yourself, "How in the world am I going to say good-bye?" since before your child started his senior year of high school, then perhaps you've built the moment into something bigger than it needs to be. If you've been constantly repeating to anyone who will listen, "I'm going to be a *wreck* when my kid leaves," or "I don't know what I'm going to *do* with myself once he's gone," then you've been conditioning yourself to assume that it's going to be a horrible, unbearable, depressing, negatively life-altering experience. And of course, you're heading straight into the land of self-fulfilling prophecy. It's really not that surprising, if you repeat something often enough, it becomes an accepted truth. Do you really want that to be your truth?

I'm not saying it's not a significant and meaningful moment. It's a big step for both of you. And because it's "big," it's easy to confuse it with "bad." But it's also the beginning of a great adventure for you and your child. And, you know, chances are you're going to see him the first time he has a holiday. As they say, this isn't "Good-bye" so much as it is "Farewell," or "See ya." You don't stop being her mother just because she's spreading her wings. It's not the end of you being a parent. And the best thing you can do as a parent is wish her well as she heads off to her next stage in life. It's just another transition. It doesn't have to be an agonizing ordeal, unless you want it to be one. It won't be, unless you make it so.

PARTING IS SUCH SWEET SORROW

So, let's just assume you've dropped off your child at the campus of choice and somehow she has managed to pry your fingers from her legs without too much of a struggle, or maybe you were discreetly escorted off the college premises by campus security. In any event, you're on your way home. You may find yourself laughing hysterically, or weeping uncontrollably. Indulge. Enjoy. *Feel.* You are entitled to any feelings that may be coming up for you. (You might want to pull the car over first.) Wallow in your emotions. You've spent the last eighteen years molding your progeny into the fine, upstanding young person he or she is today. Have at it. Let there be wailing and rending of garments and pulling of hair. Howl and keen. When else will you get a chance to keen, unless you're an Irish grandmother?

But here's a little suggestion: Avoid dramatic retellings of the day you dropped off your child at college. Your friends and colleagues may indeed be enchanted at the thought of the tears that streamed down your face as you drove the five hundred miles home, but consider sparing them. It was, no doubt, the most difficult day of your life, and no one feels as deeply as you do. About pretty much everything. You feel you are the first parent to ever leave your child at college. Perhaps we don't understand fully because, after all, the love you have for your child is beyond what most mortals feel for their children. We get that; we really do. But keep the gripping details of your parting to yourself. Don't torture your support system. Don't torture yourself, either. Let the story be your own sweet, sweet memory.

A **PEARL OF WISDOM** FOR THE CHILD WHO HAS LEFT HOME

Never, ever write anything on paper, in an instant message, a text message, or an e-mail that you wouldn't be proud of seeing splashed across the front page of your hometown newspaper.

OUTFITTING THE DORM: GIRLS AND BOYS

It is not my intention to be flippant about the actual move-in day. It is very hard work and, big picture, it is truly momentous. But as I've said elsewhere, in the spirit of remembering that perspective is your friend (and a positive perspective is your very best friend), there's no need to make it even more momentous than it already is.

It may be a *little* more momentous if you have girls rather than boys. I don't know if my particular son is some kind of monastic ascetic, but he packed for college like a true minimalist—and then, after arriving and unpacking into his new dorm room, he gave me two boxes to take back home with me. I had to convince him that keeping one extra pair of pants wouldn't be excessive. I doubt he has ever cracked either of the two special Mom boxes I packed for him (even though he's well into his first year of college as I write) containing extra vitamin C; my favorite Dr. Schulze's nutritional supplements (Echinacea Plus, SuperFood Plus On the Go, SuperTonic); an electric kettle; cold-barley tea bags and a pitcher; several sets of chopsticks (because every college freshman needs extra sets of chopsticks, right? What was I thinking? I have no idea); writing paper (*writing* paper? What are we, Amish?); extra floss and toothbrushes . . . I can't quite remember what else. Just one mother attempting to make sure her baby boy wouldn't be without his rations of Gummi Vites and seaweed snacks. He may have used the shower caddy and shampoo I got him. One hopes. Boys are . . . different.

If I'd been moving a daughter into her dorm—as many of my friends have done—the preparation would have undoubtedly been much more, um, extensive. The move-in itself: epic. One friend of mine took her daughter on one of those grand shopping sprees once they had arrived at her new Midwestern college town. You know, one of those "I'll just stop in Target and pick up a shower curtain and a few towels" kind of shopping trips, and you find yourself at the checkout stand with two overflowing shopping carts and a vague sense of having blacked out. But how in the world could anyone resist those hot-pink beanbag chairs, and that cute armoire with the foldout desk? And of course, this girl's good mama could not have left her daughter at college without first purchasing the family-size box of (wait for it) condoms. Imagine the varying hues of purple and red blooming on this girl's face as they waited in the checkout line, a jumbo box of condoms sitting atop a pile of bright bedding and a duvet. With dear mama wondering aloud, "Ribbed? Flavored? I just don't know what the kids like these days."

How much involvement in your child's dorm-room décor is too much? Outfitting the entire suite straight out of the Pottery Barn Teen catalog? Framing her posters, and then hanging them artfully around the room? Boy or girl, here's the Golden Rule: There's no need to overdo. Buying him or her a lot of stuff won't secure his or her love and loyalty, which I'm sure you figured out during his or her teenage years. There are companies that will attempt to sell you entire dorm-room outfits: fitted bedsheets, duvet covers, bath rugs, shower caddies, hampers, pillows and extra pillows, mattress pads, mattress-pad covers, bulletin boards, wastepaper baskets.

Wastepaper baskets? Really? Does your child really need that plastic hunter-green wastepaper basket that matches the plastic hunter-green hamper that matches the plastic hunter-green storage bin? No; it turns out a teenager can actually muddle through his first year of college without the bedspread matching the curtains and rugs. Nor do your children need five steamer trunks' worth of clothing and a couple of crates full of room decorations. They don't need to bring every poster they had up on their wall at home; now is the time for them to start fresh. Enough new stuff will be collected, as it should be. And when the end of the school year rolls around and you have to help them move everything out again, you will thank me.

THE CARE PACKAGE: IF I DON'T SEND ONE, DOES IT MEAN I DON'T CARE?

Just a little warning—the same outfit that sold you that complete matching bedroom set for your child's dorm is out to sell you another bill of goods: the Care Package! That's right, you'll be getting snail-mail and e-mail reminders every few weeks, just to make you feel like an extra-lousy parent for not showering your first-year college student with boxes of stuff every few months. After all, it's Groundhog Day! Doesn't your freshman need to know how much you love him on this very important holiday? Don't you need to send him a package full of . . . care?

If the boxes really were full of care and love, I'd be sending one off every day (assuming someone could lug it to the post office for me; for Pete's sake, I'm a busy girl and boxes full of love are heavy). But are these boxes really full of love for your child? No, these boxes are full of crap.

That's right, celebrate your love for your child by sending him a box full of Doritos, soda, and candy. Want to help him out during finals week? Show him how much you really care by making sure he's raising his cholesterol levels with chips and dips, and then help him stay up all night with a sugar rush from that case of Snickers bars.

Of course, you can send the "Healthy Choices Finals Pack," but I guess I'm wondering, since when did snack items become the de facto stand-in for parental love? Okay, sure, grandma baked cookies and a zillion moms since the beginning of time have used food to show how much they care. So fine, bake some cookies and send them to your student once in a while. But a regular delivery of prepackaged and processed snack items? Don't let the guilt get you.

It might be difficult resisting. You'll be seeing your progeny on the major school breaks, but if those little holidays were always important in your house—if you've always celebrated Valentine's Day at home with a heart-shaped meat loaf, red doily placemats, and chocolate hearts; if Easter means baskets of chocolate eggs, a treasure hunt, and a big ham dinner—then you may feel those heartstrings tugging when the Care Package people send those insidious little "reminders" just before Halloween and April Fool's Day.

If you really, truly feel like sending a "care" package, find a box and fill it up with personalized goodies you know your kids love. Along with a new T-shirt, perhaps, or a hat or muffler, depending on the climate of his new college home. Maybe a few articles from the newspaper (my dad and mom were always sending me articles from the newspaper), or a few photos from home.

I know, I know, who reads the newspaper anymore? Who has "photographs," when everything is downloaded on an iPhone? Well, that's sort of the point. It's a comforting, physical thing, like sending a letter. Although some of your kids may not know what a "letter" is, it does them good to receive one once in a while. And if they get a Care Package containing actual photos, written words, and cookies, it will probably strike them as a little old-fashioned, which they will probably think is totally hip and retro. It's not the only way to show you care, but it is a special way of saying, "Hey, I'm thinking of you! How ya doing?"

But go easy on the Care Packages. You don't need to send them too regularly, or it will become just another boring expected thing. Of course, if sending a Care Package will keep you from dressing up in that giant bunny suit and hand-delivering colorful, beribboned baskets to your son or daughter's dorm room, then by all means, have at it. Your children will be so grateful. Not that they don't get a big kick out of you in that bunny suit. Really.

Going Rogue

Fighting the Fear-Based Empty-Nest Cabal

IT'S ONE THING TO IDENTIFY A CHALLENGE; IT'S ANOTHER THING to create an image of the challenge as a *problem* and then live your life with this problem as its center. Just as an industry was created around the idea of being a "perfect" parent—an industry that preys upon the fears of parents, causing otherwise normal people to incessantly "enrich" their children, become "involved" to an obsessive degree, and to pay professionals to "childproof" the house—so does an industry seem to be burgeoning out of the so-called empty-nest syndrome. (And yes, that's right, here I am! Always happy to get in on the ground floor!)

The next time an empty-nest blog or an "Empty Nest Mom" suggests that "you might be feeling lonely, sad, and abandoned," run as fast as you can in the other direction. This school of thought is brought to you by the same Professional Parents who handed their lives over so happily to their children lo those many years ago. These nervous parents whose children were (and are) the center of the universe helped the parenting industry bloom, thrive, and grow into the behemoth that it has become. And now they want you to believe you're supposed to be feeling all torn up inside about your children being out of the house. Because if you were a really, truly Loving Mother, you would be.

I mean, seriously. There are support groups out there, for heaven's sake. *Support groups*, for mommies who are having a really hard time dealing with the kids being *out of the house.*

Of course, you may be feeling a little twinge of sadness, and occasionally a big one, at the fact that your child or children have moved out. It's only natural that you should miss their company from time to time. But identifying yourself as an "Empty Nest Mom" is to dwell on the Sadness, Loneliness, and Abandonment. If you *are* truly feeling those feelings, how do you expect to get to the other side if you've pegged yourself as a part of this group? I mean, how long do you think your life will be in transition if you continually identify yourself as having a "Life in Transition"? How long do you intend to *be* an "Empty Nest Mom"?

Because I swear, looking at some of these empty-nest sites, many of the bloggers look as if they're going to the grave calling themselves "Empty Nesters." They are bathing in the grief, marinating in the feelings, and happily perpetuating the sadness. They used to be the über-moms. Now they have a new job: Professional Empty Nest Parent. Join them! Their sadness is profound but they'll somehow make it through this journey, with the help of their many support groups, blogs, and chat rooms. And they encourage you to wallow with them.

This is not a "journey." Okay, fine, you can call it a journey. But make it a short one. Your kids are moving on with their lives. Don't you think you ought to do the same with yours?

WAIT ONE DARN MINUTE

Okay, does "move on with your life" sound a little harsh? I'm sorry. I really am. I know there are experts who say that "Empty Nest Syndrome" is a very real thing for a lot of parents, mostly women, and that it can descend into very real depression if left unchecked. If your child leaving for college coincides with menopause, for instance, or having to care for an ill or elderly parent, then it's no wonder that your emotions and feelings are heightened. There may be other underlying or unforeseen factors that make you feel you are spinning wildly out of control around the event.

If you're generally prone to the vapors, hate change, and tend toward panic and/or histrionics, you will certainly be doing yourself a favor by planning ahead a little. You might begin the process by imagining what life will be like with no children in the house. If the mere thought of it makes you break out in a cold sweat, then now is a good time to start figuring out your feelings. Perhaps talking to a professional will help. It may be too late to "start early"— but it's never too late to talk to a professional, if you really feel your blues are in a downward spiral.

Most of us will find ourselves at some point in our lives having to deal with extreme events and the attendant emotions. But I feel confident that most of us are built to handle the g-force of letting our children grow up, just as we learn to adjust to that big flaming ball in the sky disappearing behind the horizon every night. It's not the easiest thing for every parent. Even if you spent some quality time considering what life will be like once your darlings have left, you should still expect a bit of an adjustment period when your last child actually does fly the coop. But when that time comes, my hope is that you will be so thrilled about what you're doing with your own life that the thought of your child moving on to his next chapter will only be a source of joy, pride, and excitement about the great adventure that awaits.

3 It's Quiet. *Too* Quiet.

I KNOW, I KNOW, THEY'RE ADORABLE. AND THEY'RE YOURS. AND NOW they're away at college, never to return. Except on Spring Break, Winter Break, Presidents' Day, Thanksgiving, and three months during the summer. But still. You miss the sweet chats you used to have when he'd get home late from his math study group. You miss hearing his grudging, guttural response to your cheery "Good Morning!" You miss cleaning his hairballs out of the drain. But as wonderful as all that was, there are pros and cons to everything, and perhaps there are a few things we don't miss quite as much about living with the teen set. Perhaps, like me, you secretly don't really miss:

- Waking up early to make all those healthful and nutritious school lunches.

- Waking up early, even to make lunches that aren't all that healthful and nutritious.

- Waking up early to throw a wrapped Trader Joe's sandwich in a bag, along with a leftover piece of chocolate.

- Waking up early so you can dig through your pants pocket in search of change so your child might purchase a greasy mystery-meat pocket from the school lunch program.

- Waking up early to drive your child's school carpool.

- After your child gets his driver's license, waking up early so you can worry about him driving the school carpool.

- Waking up early, just in general.

- Receiving an annoyed "*Okaaay*, Mom," energetic rolling of the eyes, and incredulous shaking of the head after asking child to come to the dinner table for the fourth time.

- Being an Involved Parent.

- Feeling guilty over not being an Involved Enough Parent.

- Driving your child to violin and/or ballet, soccer, Little League, archery, team tennis, calculus lab, drumming circle, and the mall.

- Picking up your child from violin and/or ballet, soccer, Little League, archery, team tennis, calculus lab, drumming circle, and the mall.

- Planning your dinner parties around taking and picking up your child from violin and/or ballet, soccer, Little League, archery, team tennis, calculus lab, drumming circle, and the mall.

- Urging your child to neaten up and clean his room, several times a day.

- Cleaning your child's room several times a week.

- Exhorting your child to not leave the lights on in every room in the house.

- Turning off every light from every room your child enters and exits.

- Watching your child agonize over his homework every night.

- Agonizing over your child's homework after your child has crumpled into a tiny, crying ball.

- Sharing your bathroom.

Enough said.

The thing is, you went grocery shopping a few days ago, and there is *still food in the refrigerator*. You cleaned the house pretty thoroughly last Saturday, and it's still eerily clean. The toilet seat has miraculously stayed closed. Your nice pens are exactly where you left them yesterday! Enjoy. At least until Thanksgiving break.

4 You Never Call, You Never Write

YOU MAY FEEL AS IF YOUR CHILD IS YOUR BEST FRIEND. THIS MAY be true. This may be *more* true for you than your child, however. And so, when the time comes for your child to make that leap out of the nest, you must welcome this transition. It's a natural, positive step for him to find his place in the world.

Yes, "in the world" means outside of your house and your shared life. *Away from you.* If your child leaves home and the transition turns out to be a very easy one, this should not be a source of worry and concern. You should celebrate the fact that he is making new friends, enjoying his classes, and experiencing a lack of homesickness. This doesn't mean he doesn't love you. I know the temptation is great to repeatedly remind him that he "never calls and never writes." But don't embarrass yourself.

He never needs to know how often you pick up the phone, just to see if it's still working. And if you find yourself sending messages to him on Facebook more than once a day, because it's the only way you know how to reach him—take a deep breath. Turn those moments into moments of meditation. Meditate on your life, and what you could do with the rest of it. Eventually your child will remember his old Mom and Dad, and wonder how you're all doing. Of course, you'll be so busy living your fabulous lives he might have a hard time actually reaching you. Just tell him you'll call when you have time.

In fact, that's the point. You should be living your fabulous lives. Live your life, and let your children come to you. I don't mean play some kind of passive-aggressive game where you *pretend* to be doing more important things, in hopes that your son or daughter will then start sniffing around again because you have stopped calling them every single day. That is a terrible idea, and will only make you seem small-minded and pouty. No, I mean you should truly find things to do that interest you. Interests that don't have anything to do with your children. Interests that you can be genuinely excited about the next time you speak to your kids. Soon they will see that you really are living your life in a sincere and authentic manner, and everyone will relax, because the pressure is off.

But in the meantime, sure, it would be nice if he called once in a while, unbidden. And yes, it would be wonderful if he dropped a note, or wrote an e-mail without being asked, or pathetically begged. How do you get your kids to indulge you with a check-in? Beats me! Contrary to all the advice I just gave you above, I recently sent my son a message on Facebook. I wrote, "Darling boy: How is everything? How are your classes? You should really call or write once in a while, or we'll start thinking you don't like us." A few hours later he called. So that's one fancy technique to get your children to call

you; simply ask them. But perhaps the key is to make such requests with a light touch, and issue them very sparingly.

And what if you don't want to be the one who always calls, and always (very sparingly) asks? I asked my son if he had any ideas to help solve this dilemma. "It's just that I have a lot going on, and I don't always think of calling," he said. I told him I understood, and that yes, we both have a lot going on. We usually end up talking, one way or another; on the other hand, I told him it would be nice to hear from him more often, not just when I ask him to call. You know, a little initiative on his part would be a welcome surprise. It would show, in some small way, some thoughtfulness. Sort of like he, I don't know, cared just a little.

"Post-it notes. Maybe I could leave myself a Post-it note."

So there you have it. From one horse's mouth. On move-in day, leave your child a few packages of Post-it notes. Perhaps it would be helpful if you wrote "Call Mom!" down on each page, ahead of time. And maybe after a year of Post-it notes, calling home on a more regular basis will become a little more of a habit. A slightly more high-tech solution? Ask your young progeny to sign up for Google Calendar, find a certain day (say, Sunday) and a certain time (say, 6 p.m.) and proceed to enter the simple directive, "Call Mom!" Then, when he's at his computer writing an essay (or chatting with his friends online), up will pop a friendly reminder to check in with his dear old mother. Who is, one hopes, not pining away at home waiting for a phone call. (Have him call your cell, just in case.)

A PEARL OF WISDOM FOR THE CHILD WHO HAS LEFT HOME

Avoid getting drunk. At least avoid getting totally falling-down drunk. If you do get drunk, avoid entering a tattoo parlor. Even if you do want to take a "closer look at the priddy pictures."

BIG MAMA IS WATCHING YOU

Okay, a friend of mine has a friend who has an app on her phone that allows her to track her child. *Track her child.* And no, her "child" is not a seven-year-old who takes the subway to school every day in New York City. This is a mother who tracks her son *who is away at college.* His first year of college, and his mama is following his every move. When I heard this story, I thought to myself, "Um, does the kid know his mother is tracking him?" And the answer was, surprisingly, sadly, yes.

Are children so used to this kind of scrutiny that it doesn't seem at all odd that their moms follow them throughout the day, even from hundreds of miles away? It just seems so . . . wrong. I understand if you were expecting your child to be home at a certain hour and she doesn't show up and you can't reach her and you want to know her whereabouts and make sure she's safe and sound.

It's wonderful that we now have a technological advancement that enables us to find our kids, should they be in real trouble and need help. But, it's Friday night and you need to know what your college-age child is up to?

If your darling baby hasn't already figured out to give her cell phone to the nearest library-bound math nerd when she's on her way to party down with her posse, then I imagine that moment may soon come. But how about a little trust? How about just asking her to check in with you once in a while? If she's going on a backpacking trip or driving cross-country with a few friends, sure, tell her you'd like her to check in a little more often than you might expect her to check in from her college dorm. But try to restrain yourself from tracking her, day in and day out. Come on, it's creepy! What's next, implanting your kids with chips, so you can keep track of them for the rest of their lives?

OFFICER! I WANNA CALL MY MOMMY!

When children reach the age of consent, their parents aren't expected to be as involved in their lives. Of course we usually are, especially if we're helping them through college, or helping support them at home while they get their lives together. But either way, things are a little different when your children are over the age of eighteen. Their behavior has real consequences. If they're still doing the same kind of stupid things they enjoyed doing in high school, the consequences of their actions might haunt them for years to come. According to my friend Geri, who knows everything about the brain (and basically, everything about everything, being not only an ace speech therapist who helps brain-injured people, but a practical Midwestern girl), the adult brain doesn't really kick in until about the age of twenty-six. Unfortunately, criminal records can kick in quite a bit earlier. If your son thinks it'll be really funny to text-message a portrait of his penis to some friends, he could end up with a record as a "sex offender" for the rest of his life. So when your kids head out to that great big world or that great big college campus, they need to not only take responsibility for their health, hygiene, and finances, they need to understand how important it is to start taking real responsibility for their actions. But you've already taught them this, right? Good. Of course, it's never too late for a few gentle reminders.

5 Pets in Your Empty Nest

YOU JUST SPENT EIGHTEEN OR MORE YEARS CODDLING, DISCIPLINING, molding, supervising, feeding, caring for, enriching, and perfecting your offspring. Countless hours of your life have been devoted to every moment of your child's life. Are you sure you want to start all over with a pet?

Of course, if you've always longed for a doggie companion or a feline friend, that's another story. Get yourself to the nearest pound and find an animal buddy. But if you're considering a pet because all those empty-nest chat rooms are telling you that a pet will fill the void left by the absence of your children, you really should reconsider. This is not an ideal reason to bring an animal into your home.

Many of my friends think I'm against dogs and cats and domesticated pets in general. Not true! (Except possibly for ferrets.) But I do believe that too many people who really oughtn't to be dog owners own dogs. This has mostly to do with the fact that they keep their dogs in apartments that are too small and can't provide the kind of full attention and care I think dogs need. Their dogs become needy, neurotic, and prone to yapping.

Having a dog is a little like having a toddler for twelve years. Possibly twenty. Just like a small child, a dog will be completely dependent upon you for food, water, activities, exercise, love, and of course, its bathroom schedule. If you are truly a dog person, then you probably already have a dog. But if you are distraught over your child leaving home and think a pet will fill the void, all I'm saying is, think about it long and hard. If you really like the idea of something being completely dependent on you, then a pet might be just the thing. But if you've really been looking forward to being footloose and unfettered, understand this before you head to the local shelter: You'll need a dog-sitter every time you leave the house for more than half a day. That means no last-minute, spontaneous vacations. No sleepovers, no slumber parties, no getting in the car and just driving because you suddenly feel like seeing the Grand Canyon or the Golden Gate Bridge . . . which you can't really afford to do anymore anyway, now that you've got to pay that six-hundred-dollar vet bill. And of course, there are a few other unexpected expenses, like regular carpet cleaning, professional pet training, and that dog psychologist the nice lady at the dog rescue place told you was essential for the mental health of your newly adopted friend.

The idea of having a loving, furry, loyal pal can be a romantic one, and it's not that I generally encourage pessimism, but it might be wise to think about everything that could possibly go wrong before you welcome a pet into your life.

On the other hand, you may already have a pet in your nest. That adorable puppy your children had to have when they were tweens is still an energetic, bounding ball of dog love. He's only about seven years old, and your kids have both moved on to college, or other pursuits. Chances are you've been the one doing most of the caring for the animal since the pet was first procured; and you are either already a fan of dogs and/or cats and/or guinea pigs or you are bitter, resentful, and hopeful that an unfortunate "accident" might befall your unintentional animal boarder. You have become, by default, a person with a pet. The kids are gone, and now you've got another five to ten years of taking care of their animals, depending on the type of animal and its life expectancy. I pray your children did not acquire a grey parrot or a tortoise, or you are in it for the long haul. Of course, you can always pawn them off on the grandchildren in another twenty years.

Then again, pets can be nice to have around. Dog lovers will tell you (and anyone who will listen) that dogs provide companionship, comfort, and a warm body for your feet at night. A dog will also provide a host of psychological benefits (which I am not psychologically equipped to explain, not being a dog owner). Suffice to say, dogs are apparently good for your feelings of well-being. For the true dog lover, they are just another adored member of the family, supplying years of cheer, unconditional love, and loyalty. Not to mention all the exercise you'll get walking them four times a day.

Cats, however, in my opinion, are an acquired taste. Let's face it: You really won't be getting much in return for loving a cat. It's kind of a one-way street. After enduring your child's teen years, you may be used to this kind of relationship, in which case, a cat is the perfect choice. And so long as you leave food and a litter box in easy reach, your cat really won't notice if you leave town for a few days. She might even let you pet her when you return home.

I AM SIMPLY DEVASTATED THAT MY CHILD HAS GONE! REALLY. REALLY, I AM.

All right, admit it. Some of you really are not all that heart-broken about your child leaving the nest. Am I right? Oh come on, you can tell me. I know, I know, you have to put on the Sad Mom face to keep up appearances, but secretly you're wondering what the hell is wrong with these parents who seem like broken shells of their former selves now that Junior has gone off to pursue a higher education. They talk about missing their children all day, every day. And you think they're kind of, well, insane.

It's not just you, really. And I'm here to tell you that it's okay to feel jubilant, possibly giddy, at the thought of your child leaving home. In fact, I think it's a very healthy reaction. "Wait a minute," you might be saying, with that kind of squinty look you get. "In what way are you quali-fied to tell me that it's a healthy reaction? Maybe I'm an insensitive, uncaring she-monster without a human bone in my body!"

Well, actually, I am qualified by the mere fact that I am feeling the very same way. That's right, a slightly jubilant sensation is occurring. And do I look like an insensitive, uncaring she-monster? Perhaps sometimes, very early in the morning, before coffee. The rest of the time, perfectly agreeable. And in fact, a very proud mama. One child has successfully cleared the launch pad, and I am counting the years, days, hours, and minutes until my youngest will be out of the house. (Literally! 1,239 days, 29,737 hours, 1,784,265 minutes! It's a heady feeling.)

Granted, it could be that I'm counting the days because my youngest is, at the moment, a rather monosyllabic, moody teen. A cliché of a teen. A grunting, contrary, often snappish teen. In short, I must share my house with an insufferable teen who leaves crusty dishes lying about, no matter what anyone might say. This may change, one hopes, when he reaches his senior year, at which time I may become all warm and fuzzy and despondent at the thought of him leaving. But in the meantime, I confess I daydream about the entirely empty nest that awaits, just around the bend. I will be the last to blame you for feeling a little excited about the prospect yourself.

Just try to pretend once in a while, for the sake of the children. They might get a little miffed to find out how much you're enjoying life without them. It could hurt their feelings if they knew the truth about how long you've been plotting that room makeover and that trip to the Bahamas. So try to sound all choked up on the phone, once in a while. Tell them how much you miss them, and try not to appear too excited when they tell you they won't be hanging around the house all summer long because they got an internship for their summer break.

On the other hand, don't be surprised if your feelings of jubilation and giddiness give way to some confusing feelings of real sadness. You might end up grieving just a little for the end of an era, if not for the stinky teen who never picked up his socks. Maybe even for the stinky teen, you never know. Be prepared for all possibilities. Celebrate your jubilation and be ready to honor your grief. And then move on—happily—to the next part of your life.

A QUICK NOTE TO THE CHILD
WHO HAS BEEN LEFT BEHIND

Honestly, sweetie, I didn't think you'd actually *read* that. I mean, you so rarely pick up books anymore. But what I meant was, I am counting the days, hours, and minutes before you leave because . . . well, I'm just so excited that you'll be starting *your* next chapter in life. After high school. Which you still haven't started. Yet. So! Yes, looking forward to that. But also planning to savor every single little moment of the next four years of living with you.*

*If you still have one more little darling left at home who hasn't yet finished high school and left the nest, well, just remember: They need their independence too. They can't be stand-ins for their older brothers and sisters who have already left. You must try to not pin on the youngest child whatever hopes may have been dashed regarding the older siblings. He is his own person. Yes, they all tend to have seemingly the same stinky socks, but they are individuals, nonetheless, and should be treated individually. And sweetie, if you're still there? I think the garbage needs taking out. Thanks. And don't tell your brother about the new sewing room, just yet. xo

part 2

Hello, Gorgeous!

6 And You Are . . . ?

PERHAPS YOU'VE NOTICED THE CONSPICUOUS ABSENCE OF children draped around the furniture and setting up shop in front of the television just when you want to sit down and watch your favorite news shows. Take a look around. You'll see, perhaps, that the area near the toaster you swept clean just this morning is *still* free of crumbs. And what's this? There appears to be a dearth of dirty dishes sitting on various tables and desktops. You haven't found a single piece of half-eaten pizza under the sofa—for weeks.

And that man, sitting across from you at the breakfast table . . . he looks . . . familiar. You know you know him, you just don't know how.

If you have spent the last eighteen years in your minivan driving your kids to soccer practice, helping them build solar-powered mousetraps for the science fair, and volunteering in the classroom, you might vaguely remember that you probably embarked upon this whole "having children" idea with another person. But the last time you remember saying more than a few words to your significant other, you were asking him to "please hold the baby so I can eat my dinner." You've been through thick and thin together, and look! He's still here! Say hello to your spouse. It's time to get reacquainted.

There are a lot of fun ways to refamiliarize yourself with your spouse, now that the house is free of younger people. First of all, there's no one left at home to remind you how old you really are. And age is a very relative thing, isn't it? I mean, how do you really feel? About twenty-five, I'd guess, despite that crampy leg and thinning hair.

Sure it's the same old house, but when was the last time you felt comfortable wandering about in your underpants with a lit joint in your hand? Even if you don't smoke pot, you never have smoked pot, or you quit before you graduated from college, why not give it another try? Because you *can*—not that you want to make a habit of it. You *can* stay up until four in the morning watching movies. You *can* fall asleep on the sofa, fully clothed. You *can* eat cereal and Pop-Tarts for dinner. You can have friends over on a school night and *make noise*.

In the past, you may have not felt completely at ease doing naked dances in the living room, knowing there were children in the house. But now you can express yourself freely without fear of impressionable youngsters wondering what the hell Mom is getting up to with the scarves and the feathers. You may once again loudly indulge in your personal at-home tributes to Bessie Smith. Your baton twirling will no longer be a source of derision and hilarity. And of course, the obvious: There are no more limitations on when or where you can engage in sexual activities with your partner. That's right, wild sex on the living room sofa, on the dining room table, or on the kitchen floor after breakfast is no longer out of the question. It may be horribly uncomfortable, and you may not love the feel of the cold, hard floor, or the way the handcuffs scratch the finish, but there's freedom in knowing you can do those things, any hour of the day.

And when you've finished brushing the crumbs and dust bunnies off the backs of your bare thighs, there are other things you can do. Start making plans with your partner. Your partner may not be the type of person who makes plans. He may the kind of person who believes that if you don't have the money to tour the world for a year, then you shouldn't bother talking about it. Well, there are several reasons why you *should* talk about it. For one thing, by talking about your hopes, dreams, and ideas for the future, you may actually make those dreams come true.

Plus, your partner has no idea what he's missing. Sure, traveling is fun, but planning your trip is sometimes the biggest part of the fun. Planning imaginary trips is equally fun, and can provide hours of entertainment for you and your partner. And face it: You're going to be together a lot for the next god-knows-how-many years. Together, just the two of you, with no children around. You'll need to find a few things to do together. (Besides the aforementioned sex on the kitchen floor, etc. Because after all: ouch! Plus, you know how clean that kitchen floor is.) Planning for your future and sharing your dreams is one of those things you can enjoy together. Make a wish list of your dream future. What is it you really want to do in the next bunch of years? What is it your partner really wants to do? Perhaps there will be some crossover. Let's hope so.

If you've got a lot of things on your to-do list, and your partner
has a whole lot of things he wants to do that have nothing to do
with what you want to do, you needn't give up on your dreams. Nor
do you need to give up on your marriage. Let's say you both like to
travel, but you're very different kinds of travelers. For instance, I
have a big fat plan to move to Paris and live on a small river barge
for a year, with the intention of traveling the rivers and canals of
France and possibly a few other countries. My husband is the kind
of traveler who likes to get to the airport four hours before a flight,
who doesn't like to get lost, and who likes to be comfortable. I don't
believe he would ever put "live on a river barge for a year" on his
list of "Things I Must Do." So my plan is to simply arrange everything ahead of time. That way, we can both enjoy the adventure.
I'll figure out how to acquire the barge—I *like* to do that sort of
thing (yes, control issues)—and I'll set everything up so that when
he arrives, he'll find a cozy little home all ready to move in, and—
most important—a cozy little spot to do his crossword puzzles.

I figure, someone who doesn't like to get lost might find traveling
by river a safer bet than traveling by ocean. I mean, you pretty much
go up the river and down the river. How lost can you get? And
we'll have a handy map to tell us the name of each town as we pass
through. If it looks nice, we can decide together whether or not we
want to stop and sample the local cheese and wine for a few weeks.

Life is just too short to spend much more of it curled up on a
sofa watching television. And new technology makes it easy to live
pretty much anywhere in the world. My husband can watch his
basketball and baseball via the Internet on whatever new device

happens to be the current rage. We can keep up on all our favorite news and politics, without the temptation to throw things—because while throwing things at the TV provides some perverse satisfaction, throwing things at an iPad just seems pathetic. And why would we want to throw things anyway? We'll be floating on a river, eating French cheese.

While in Paris, I can wander the halls of the Louvre for hours on end and get lost in the Marais whenever the fancy strikes. My husband can sit in his comfy spot on deck and do his sudoku, or saunter to his favorite cafe for a baguette and an espresso. We can invite friends to stay with us, so we can get a dose of the English language. And when we're ready to move on, we can take turns at the wheel and look at our map, and decide whether we want to go to Sweden, Bordeaux, or Spain. And whether we should encourage the children to visit us during the summer.

Now, you might be thinking I'm painting a rather romantic picture of how I imagine my life after the kids have moved out. And it's possible I have. Tomorrow I might hatch another plan, to live in a yurt on Maui, or travel the east coast of the United States by bicycle. And then I'll figure out how I might make the idea sound appealing to that vaguely familiar-looking man sitting across the breakfast table.

A **PEARL OF WISDOM** FOR THE CHILD WHO HAS LEFT HOME

Okay, I'd prefer it if you didn't drink. You got drunk, didn't you? Okay, but remember, do not ever, *ever* get into a car with someone who's been drinking. And for every alcoholic beverage you drink, drink at least one glass of water. Oh, and take two aspirin and eat a banana before you go to sleep. Potassium!

Surely You Have Something to Do?

7

YOU DON'T HAVE TO TACKLE FOREIGN PORTS TO REKINDLE A SENSE of shared adventure with your significant other; a good road trip is another great way to get reacquainted. Travel by train or pack up the car and explore parts of your own country you've never seen. It's likely been a long time since you've taken an obligation-and-child-free trip together, or maybe, come to think of it, you never have. If planning an expedition like this sounds daunting, then simply think of a theme, and then plan your trip around that theme. Tour the national parks, or historic baseball parks. Take a road-food trip across the country, stopping at out-of-the-way diners and roadside eateries. Close your eyes, stick pins in a map, and go to the spots they hit. Research local offbeat museums along the way, or go across country entirely on back roads and old highways.

If neither one of you has any desire to travel at all, there are plenty of other activities that can stand in for a good road trip. Date nights are fun, but how about turning your date nights into an interesting learning experience? Find a weekly night class to take together. If one of you wants to take a course in Architectural Landscape and your partner prefers a class in Short Fiction Writing, then take turns. Let your partner choose the first class, and you can choose the next.

Make a list of all the free things you can do in your city or town. Even if you can afford regular fancy nights out, you will unearth a whole new world of things to do once you start discovering free and inexpensive events. Concerts in the park. Community theater. People watching in a part of town you don't usually visit. Get out of your comfort zone. Try some interesting hole-in-the-wall restaurants, and/or cuisines from countries with names you can't pronounce. Date nights don't always have to be about eating out, but when you do go out to dinner together, a nice date doesn't always have to involve white-tablecloth service and sommeliers.

For that matter, why not take some cooking classes together? Perhaps the "cook" of the family does not relish (so to speak) the idea of being the "cook" for the next twenty years. Perhaps that person would like someone else to take the reins in the kitchen once in a while. But maybe the "cook" knows that he or she is destined to be the "cook" for the next twenty years unless the idea of eating pizza, takeout, and frozen entrees every night is appealing. Cooking classes are the perfect solution. Your significant other may not have ever had any desire to learn how to cook, but I bet he likes to eat. And enjoying a good meal might be just the right incentive to enroll in that first cooking class.

If you're the kind of couple who rarely entertained during your child-rearing years, why not start having regular gatherings? You and your partner might see different facets of each other around different groups of your friends.

I have some pals who decided to hold monthly wine-tasting parties, because a group of them all want to learn more about wine. What they don't know about wine they make up for in passion and curiosity. It's an enthusiasm-based wine tasting group. Honestly, there is no better jumping-off point than enthusiasm, for just about any endeavor. And because wine is often misunderstood to be exclusively the purview of elite, magically knowledgeable wine experts, some people hesitate to voice their opinions on the subject. My friend Beth von Benz (who has the enviable job of being a wine expert in New York City) says that learning about wine is very much like learning a new language, or any new skill. It has to be practiced. But as Beth says, "I'd rather practice drinking wine than conjugate irregular Spanish verbs, right?" And she's got a point.

You could start a book group with your partner, if you're both readers. Or have a regular Movie Night with a group of friends. Or a Bad Movie Club, where you rotate houses with a few friends for the purpose of enjoying all the bad movies that have ever been made. *The Claw*, anyone? If you both like to work with your hands, plan a project both of you would enjoy working on with results you will equally enjoy: refurbish your patio, start a vegetable or flower garden, create a sculpture for your backyard or balcony. A regular physical activity you and your partner can do together would be good for both of you. You know it would, don't make that face. If the idea of taking up tennis is too daunting, how about paddle tennis, which doesn't require quite the skill or killer backhand. Ping-pong? You and your partner could start hiking, or kayaking. Even a daily walk to the park or the local coffeehouse would be better than doing nothing.

If all goes well, you will rediscover what possessed you to want to make babies with this person in the first place. You may have both changed over the years, but more often than not it's fun to discover that the person with whom you've been sharing a bed and a dining room table all these years still has the same fine qualities you fell in love with those many years ago.

FOR THE SINGLE PARENT

If you've raised your child or children as a single parent, your empty nest may feel extra empty. It's probably only been this quiet one or two times in your life, like maybe when you got all the kids off to summer camp during the same two-week period. Two whole weeks. You had to work the entire time they were gone, but still, the thrill of those few hours alone every night has never left you. And you've dreamed about having a little "alone time" ever since. But now here you are. If a door slams in the middle of the night, you've either got ghosts or are experiencing a break-in. If there's a mess in the kitchen or a trail of crumbs leading into the TV room, you know it's your mess and your crumbs. And it's kind of a bummer that you're the only one around who can take out the garbage.

But as I continue to proclaim, there is a positive side to your situation: Whatever you decide to do with your time from here on out, you only have to answer to yourself. If you have always wanted to kayak across the English Channel, there's no one to tell you that it's a bad idea. Now is the time to make a list of all the harebrained things you have been longing to do since you changed that first diaper. Perhaps they won't sound so harebrained after all. And your ideas will be yours and yours alone; no compromises necessary. Your dream of living on a sampan off the coast of Java for six months won't have to magically transform into an all-inclusive luxury cruise in the Bahamas, just because your significant other prefers a little more pampering than might be available on a rustic seagoing vessel.

On the other hand, if you would prefer to simply enjoy your solitude, putter around the garden, occasionally go out on a date—and enjoy the kids when they come home for holidays—then you've got no one around to tell you to drag your sorry butt off the sofa and do something. Just make sure the solitude of a child-free house doesn't become *too* comfortable. The company of others is good for our mental health. Other people give us fresh perspectives on life. We're social animals, and it's good for us to have friends, friends to laugh with and cook for. If you're naturally a homebody, it's all too easy to become a little too housebound in the absence of a maelstrom of kids' activities. And before you know it, you're feeding stray cats and sleeping in the same sweatpants you wore for the last few days. From there, it's just a short step to becoming the crazy lady down the street who chats with invisible people and saves newspapers.

So if you like the single life, but find yourself with a little too much "alone time," find a hiking group, a rowing club, a gardening club. Get out of the house. Meet your neighbors. Think of a place you've always wanted to visit and join a tour group. Create your own tour group with a handful of other single parents you might know. Join Facebook, if you haven't already. I know, it's virtual and imaginary and a giant time-waster, but it does enable you to connect with friends. (And you can check on your kid's Facebook page while you're there.)

8 You and Yourself

Love with a Beautiful Stranger

GETTING TO KNOW EACH OTHER AGAIN AS A COUPLE AFTER SO many years of raising kids and relating in a busy family dynamic is one of the great silver linings of the empty nest. But this doesn't mean you must spend every waking moment with your significant other, now that the two of you are on your own. You will quite likely also need a little time apart from one another, to explore individual pursuits and discover a few personal passions. This can be a very positive thing, and should not be an indication that you want to be away from your spouse. Discovering and stoking your passions outside the house doesn't mean you don't love your partner. Your interests and enthusiasms shouldn't be a threat to each other, even if one of you doesn't have as many—or the same—outside interests. At the same time you are exploring the pleasures of a new era of courtship with your partner, the time has come to renew the pleasures of privacy and lavish some attention on yourself. It might appear that you're having an affair, but you are simply having an affair with yourself.

Having an affair with yourself can be an exciting, heady experience, especially if this is the first time you've ever done that sort of thing. I mean, there you are, raising kids—driving them to Little League one minute and taking them to college the next. And then one day you walk past the mirror, look into your beautiful eyes, and say, "Well, hello, stranger! What can I do for you?" And you will discover that you are really good at something you never knew you were, or there's something you used to be really good at that you really miss doing, like you want to train for a marathon, or you have a hankering to start a business. If you have been a stay-at-home parent, you may have a yearning to start up work again. If you have been working full-time, you may suddenly have a yen to take some time off and paint watercolors, or hike the Appalachian Trail.

If your spouse has never had any desire to hike to the grocery store, much less the Appalachian Trail, he may think your reason for wanting to take a hike is because you want to be far, far away from him, when the truth is, you just really want to hike the Appalachian Trail. He may not understand why anyone would want to do such a thing. Does this mean you shouldn't do it? Well, that's between you, yourself, and your spouse. Your skeptical partner might be more inclined to embrace the idea if you include him or her in the planning process. Including him in your research should demystify the whole "I'm hiking the Appalachian Trail" idea and help your partner gain an understanding of your need to take on a personal challenge.

(Of course, if you're really meeting your hot Venezuelan mistress and going nowhere near the Appalachian Trail, then that could be a problem. Having an affair with yourself might feel vaguely threatening to your spouse, but if you really are having an affair with, you know, *another person*, then, um, you really ought to sort things out before your marriage explodes.)

Your spouse—and possibly some friends and family members—may not understand why in the world you've taken up this new pursuit. They may not appreciate this newfound passion you've developed. Maybe they just don't understand the "new you." If you decide to start training for a marathon when you and your spouse have always been enthusiastic couch potatoes, he or she may take it as a personal affront, and you may not necessarily get the moral support you'd hoped for. Family members can balk when we don't play out the role they have always had us pegged for. "What do you mean you've decided to join a pottery collective and start an apprenticeship in Old Master glazing? *I'm* the Creative One, *you're* the Suburban Mom!" Sometimes it can chip away at your confidence when those around you aren't embracing your new passion with the same kind of fervor that you are. But don't let the wet blankets dissuade you from doing what you have to do.

Enjoy the excitement you're feeling about your new endeavor. Share your enthusiasm. Chances are when your spouse sees how happy you are pursuing all those exciting outside interests, he may want to find a few of his own. Or he may want to join in on a few of yours. Hey, you're having an affair with yourself, after all. Who could blame him for wanting to get in on the action?

Beyond the Empty Nest

Before the Parade Passes By

YOU'VE DONE SUCH A GOOD JOB RAISING YOUR KIDS. THEY DID well in school, and now they're moving on to college. It's been a hectic couple of decades.

Wait—*decades?* Has it really been that long? Weren't you meaning to start that novel when your youngest was just starting middle school? You started taking notes for it about ten years ago, but you just never had the time to sit down and write. And it was always your intention to go back to art school, you've just been too busy. And it would have been nice to do that walking tour in England . . . but maybe next year would be a better time. After all, you want to be here when your child comes home for winter break. And spring break. And summer break.

There's always been a good reason to put off personal projects, of course. Just too much going on. But now you've got your life stretched out in front of you. Maybe you can't quit work while your kids are in college, and maybe you feel you need to stick around and be there for them once they've graduated college and are launching their own lives. Now that they're away at college, perhaps you feel as if you'd be abandoning them, if you moved out of their childhood home. Even if they do only visit three times a year. Eventually there may be weddings to plan, or grandchildren to help watch over. Eventually your college graduate will need curtains for his new apartment. Your youngest may want to go to graduate school, and of course you'll have to help out. Your dream of setting sail to Tahiti is going to have to wait one more time, there's just too much to do. Where the hell does the time go?

Of course, as we get older, our priorities change. Some of our dreams have naturally fallen by the wayside. In some cases there are reasons why that book never got finished—like the one written completely in iambic pentameter. And thankfully for all your friends and family, you lost interest in the banjo, and never really took to the clarinet the way you thought you might. Sometimes the things we thought we had to do before we left this mortal coil turn out to be things we just don't feel like doing so much, anymore.

For instance, around the time I turned forty, I took a bunch of sailing lessons—because I had never learned to sail, because I wanted to see if I could actually do it, and because the idea of sailing from Los Angeles to Hawaii seemed challenging and romantic (I'm a little bit of a sucker for challenges and romance). I loved learning how to sail, and felt very proud when I got my navigation certificate from the Coast Guard. I enjoyed learning how to provision a boat and set a course during my four-day Coastal Cruising class. Of course, that annoying seasickness problem still needs to be overcome. But all in all, every class from my very first day of Sailing 101 was a wonderful experience.

Nevertheless, I can't say that I still have a burning desire to plot my course to Hawaii. Once you start learning something, you realize how little you know about it, and sometimes that means recalculating the pros and cons, the trade-offs and payoffs of a goal. I'm not saying that I'll never sail to Hawaii, but that dream is no longer on the top of my list. The experience did, however, get me thinking about living on a boat, and that is definitely at the top of my list. So yes, our hopes and dreams mutate and evolve over the years. So it's always a good idea to check in with yours, and see how they're faring. You do not want to be eighty years old, explaining to your grandchildren that you were "always too busy" to do that thing you had hoped to do your entire life. On the other hand, maybe you don't mind if you never do that thing. Maybe you realized at some point that the reason you were put on this earth was so you could raise good children and send some fine, well-adjusted adults out into the world. Heaven knows we need more of those.

But perhaps you've been so consumed with your children's lives— and are still just as consumed even as they grow into adulthood— that you've put your own dreams on hold. Now is the time to search your heart and meditate on what really matters to you. Have you taken on any new challenges lately? Are you avoiding taking on new challenges because you're stuck in a rut, or because you're truly enjoying your current life? Take a look at your routine, and imagine the same routine ten years from now, or twenty years from now. Does the thought of waking up in the same house every morning and watching the same TV every night make you feel comforted, or does it trigger your fight-or-flight response? Do you break out in hives at the idea of going to the same grocery store and seeing the same handful of people at the same dinner parties for the rest of your life?

Or maybe you're deeply involved in your community, and you can't imagine ever leaving the place you've been living for the last umpteen years. You just can't imagine living anywhere but the town where you brought up your kids. Maybe you really have found contentment, and you've truly got that "I'm home" feeling every time you walk through the door of your house, or go to your favorite park or restaurant. You may already be doing exactly what you always dreamed of doing. And if you know it, then you're extremely lucky. You may be exactly where you want to be already. But just check in with yourself and make sure you really have done everything you ever wanted to do.

Not all of us want to climb Everest, and good thing, too; the place is crowded enough. But attaining even simple goals is good for your mental health, and can be most satisfying. How long has it been since you were able to curl up with a good book—and finish it? How often have you thought that you'd like to catch up on your classics? Have you ever hoped to read *Ulysses,* or the Penguin translations of Proust's *In Search of Lost Time*? Or everything Tolstoy ever wrote? Have you ever wanted to make your own bread, even if you only do it once? Have you ever imagined riding a motorcycle across the country, or maybe just to get your groceries? How about tooling around town on an Italian scooter? How about taking ballet from a local studio? You may not become the principal dancer of the

New York City Ballet—at least in this lifetime—but you'll be taking your mind and body out for a spin, and that kind of movement is good for both. Have you ever wanted to learn to knit, or do needlepoint? Okay, me neither, but you never know, many find it restful and meditative.

The point is, you don't need to tackle an extreme or impossible-seeming task to feel as if you've lived a full life or done a few interesting things. Once the children embark upon their own lives, you just can't give up on your own, only living vicariously through them. For the sake of your brain, you need to keep stretching it. You need to keep taking on little challenges. And maybe you need to take a good hard look at the life you want to look back on fondly, ten or twenty years from now. What is it you have always wanted to do, and what are you waiting for?

A SLIGHTLY CREEPY EXERCISE
THAT MIGHT JUST WORK

Okay, this isn't my idea, unless you really like it; then it's totally my idea. But I was reading an article by a woman, Roz Savage is her name, who, at the age of thirty-eight, rowed across the Atlantic Ocean by herself. She also . . . wait a minute, what? Yes, that's right, I said rowed. As in "row, row, row your boat." She *rowed* a seagoing kayak-canoe-type contraption across the ocean. And then she took on the Pacific Ocean, and then moseyed over to the Indian Ocean, and tackled that one. Yawn. Anyway, before she accomplished these Herculean feats, she performed a small, interesting experiment: She wrote two obituaries for herself.

I know, I know, we don't want to think about death. Well, I hate thinking about taxes and melting glaciers, but there you are. Roz wrote two versions of her own obituary. One celebrated the life she wanted; it was the obituary of a "risk taker," a celebration of a life filled with (and I love the way she put this) "spectacular successes and failures." Spectacular failures! No one ever talks about how important spectacular failures are, when looking at a complete, well-lived life. The other obituary was her life the way she saw herself headed; dull, conventional, barely worth a second glance if you were reading it in the newspaper.

The upshot is, she decided that rowing across the ocean was exactly the kind of project she needed to make her life complete. Maybe after writing a dream obituary for yourself you might discover that you're meant to join the Peace Corps, or move to a small town and raise goats, or start a bakery, or become a cheese maker, or a surf instructor, or an international mediator. So why not give it a try? Write your own obituary. One that reflects your life the way you've lived it so far and the direction you see it heading. The other describing the person you always wanted to be. Then see how the two match up. Maybe it'll help give you some clues as to the kinds of challenges you might want to undertake, or experiences you might want to experience, before that obituary goes to press.

A **PEARL OF WISDOM** FOR THE CHILD WHO HAS LEFT HOME

Learn one good magic trick. One you can do with a deck of cards. Because there is not one person who is not charmed and amused by a good card trick. (Except for this one friend of mine who *hates* magic tricks. She used to date a magician. The thing is, she ended up marrying this other guy who is a genius at card tricks. So whenever we visit them, we have to sneak him off to another room to do some magic for us. And it is sublime. So, seriously, learn some card tricks, *most* people love them.)

HERE'S A TIP, MS. LONELY, PINING MOTHER

If you really miss the constant activity and the sound of young voices in the house that much, then go volunteer in a kids' playground or a local community center. I bet your local preschool or elementary school would love to have you help out in the classroom, and would so appreciate you giving of your time, your skills, and your energy. Remember back when your kids were younger, how much fun it was to read to the first-graders, and the second-graders? And how all the kids used to run after you in the playground, and the girls wanted to hold your hand and they'd squeal with delight when they saw you coming and laugh when you did those funny voices? Remember the awed faces as you shook up that jar of cream and it miraculously turned into butter? (Hello, Pioneer Days!) You can experience that kind of adulation and unconditional love again, by being a volunteer. Yes, you can be an elementary school celebrity once again. And then perhaps your days will not feel so bleak.

From Chopsticks to Concertos

SOME OF US SAW ONE OR MORE OF OUR CHILDREN THROUGH YEARS of piano, clarinet, violin, cello, trumpet, tuba, bassoon, aeolian harp, harmonium, kalimba, and/or flutophone. If you were a committed Suzuki parent, then you spent the last decade, more or less, deeply involved in your child's musical education. Every last "Twinkle" variation is indelibly imprinted on your cerebral cortex, and you can hum Vivaldi sonatas in your sleep.

But now that your young prodigy is off to Juilliard or Berklee, or perhaps attending a state college on a nice little music scholarship, you find that you really miss the strains of Bach and Haydn wafting through the hallway at night.

It might not have occurred to you, but you're already halfway to becoming a concert (or at least living room) pianist or violinist or cellist yourself. You know the drill! You've studied the repertoire! You took countless notes, written and mental, on technique and form all those years when your child was learning the rudiments of his instrument! At this point, it really is only a matter of getting yourself an instrument and digging up your child's first music books. Just because you never took lessons as a child doesn't mean it's too late. Okay, learning to read music and play an instrument will not be as easy as it might've been at the age of seven, but it's not impossible. And I'm not kidding when I say you are halfway there. First of all, you are not seven years old. Half your lesson won't be spent trying to keep you focused, and the other half trying to get you to keep your feet planted on the floor. More important, you won't have to attend school while learning how to efficiently operate a complex musical instrument.

Music is just the nicest thing to have around the house. And it truly is a universal language. Bring a musical instrument anywhere, and you'll have an instant party. Even if you've decided to pick up one of the more classical instruments, like cello or violin, it's not as difficult as you might think to add some easy folk songs and Irish music to your repertoire, once you learn the basics.

You could invite your more musical friends over to the house for monthly Music Nights. If you're a little shy about singing, then singing with friends might help you out of your shell. A certain husband I know organizes the occasional "Beatles Night." All Beatles. All the time. Because everyone knows at least one Beatles song. And those who know only one are usually happy to listen to the others. If you've already been getting together with a few friends and playing music in your garage every Sunday, you might be ready to start your own midlife garage band. Just think, no sullen, superior teenagers at home to make fun of you! You can jam for hours! Host a few friends with a few bottles of wine and call it a gig!

Even people who aren't particularly musically minded enjoy singing along to classic campfire songs. If you never went camping as a child and don't know any campfire songs, well, maybe now's the time to learn some. And, by the way, if you really didn't go camping as a child, I am very sad for you, and highly encourage you try it out sometime. And what better time than now? If only so you can know the joy of singing "You Are My Sunshine" around a campfire. And s'mores. And shivering in the dark to ghost stories, and sleeping in a sleeping bag, and making coffee in the open air. But perhaps that's for another chapter.

11 Happy Trails

Didn't I Tell You to Go Camping?

THAT'S RIGHT; YOU SAID YOU'VE NEVER BEEN CAMPING, AND I SAID, "What the hell?" And then you told me that no one had ever taken you camping, and that you don't even own a sleeping bag—in fact, you've never seen the inside of a tent. Nor do you really go outside much. And then I said, "What the hell?" again. Because that probably means you never took your kids camping.

But okay, fine, it's not the end of the world. But you really ought to try it sometime, like, before you're ninety-two. Why? Because! Because it'll get you out of your normal routine, because it'll get you outdoors and into nature, because you'll never taste coffee as delicious as the cup you drink on a chilly morning when you're camping. Because you'll learn how to cook over a campfire, and make s'mores. Because you might get to pee in the woods. Because you might see a bear, or a lizard. Because food tastes different when you're camping. Because you will see a *bazillion* stars at night, and you'll get that weird whooshing sound in your head as you look up at the stars, and you'll start feeling very tiny, and wonder what infinity feels like, and, like, whoa. *There are a bazillion stars*, and then you'll see your first shooting star, and you'll want to stay up all night so you can see another. Because you can eat a chocolate bar for breakfast. Because you might catch a fish, and if you do, you can roast it on a stick and eat it. Because you'll smell smells you've never smelled. Because you need to know what it's like to sleep in a sleeping bag. Because you can sing and tell ghost stories at night around a campfire. Because it's fun!

There are different levels of camping, by the way, in case you don't think you're up for hiking the Himalayas and sleeping at Mount Everest's base camp. There are alternatives to building an ice cave on the side of a mountain. There are options aside from slogging a twenty-pound backpack through a buggy backwoods. On the other hand, driving a thirty-foot luxury RV to a crowded campground doesn't really count as camping. So what does? Well, according to me, camping can be anything that gets you out into the great outdoors, where you stay for a few days or longer without the aid of electricity, running water, generators, computers, or a flat-screen TV. Which means anything from car camping at a campground (where you park next to your campsite instead of packing in; you'll sleep in a tent, but you can bring a blow-up mattress, a cooler full of imported cheeses, and a case of Prosecco for your camping enjoyment) to backpacking in a national park (which means if you want that five-pound wheel of Cheddar and an assortment of wines, you'll have to carry them on your back) to any number of fantastic and relatively luxurious camping packages on offer at various national parks and campgrounds across the country.

There are fifty-eight national parks in the United States. Apart from the obvious, like Yellowstone and Yosemite, there are parks known for their canyons, volcanoes, hot springs, geysers, mountain peaks, deserts, sand dunes, caverns, caves, reefs, mangroves, lakes, rivers, glaciers, and redwood forests, stretching from Alaska to Florida. Waiting to be discovered, in case you never got around to that when you were busy raising kids. And if you don't think you're up for sleeping in a tent under the stars, it's not difficult to find comfortable lodgings near these natural wonders. Lodgings with actual doors, beds, and running water. An enclosed and cozy perch from where you can venture out during the day to stun yourself with a little nature.

A wonderfully charming way to get you and your (perhaps reluctant) partner acclimated to the idea of living and dining outdoors is to have a picnic. Okay, there is no actual sleeping outside involved, unless you take a nice afternoon nap on your picnic blanket. But a good picnic will give you the sense of provisioning for a trek outdoors, even though that trek may only be for half a day.

You'll want some good grub, of course, which can be anything from the simplest hard-boiled eggs and celery sticks to roast chicken and pasta salad to the sky's the limit. You can picnic just about anywhere, and the spot you choose will help you decide whether you want to bring iced tea, bottled water, or a bottle of wine. A local beach, or the mountains a little farther afield? A picnic by nature should be easy, fairly comfortable, and not involve hours of driving, or you really will end up on a camping trip. For that matter, you can practice picnicking at a local park, or in your own backyard. There's no Picnic Rule Book that requires picnics must occur only on bucolic, far-off hillsides. The advantage of having a backyard picnic, of course, is that you can easily run inside for more wine.

And maybe in the middle of finishing your second bottle, you and your spouse will start planning a real camping trip, or think about renting a cabin on a lake for a week sometime. Camping isn't all about bugs and discomfort, really. And maybe after getting a few camping trips under your belt, you'll plan one with your kids. Even if the kids are now in their twenties, you'll be able to attest to the fact that it's never too late to go camping.

ONE HUSBAND'S GUIDE
TO COUNTERACTING EMPTY NEST SYNDROME

Some people have no problem with Empty Nest Syndrome and don't understand why their spouse is looking for all these activities to fill the time. As far as they're concerned, all of the time that used to be spent being a parent can now be spent, well, having sex. Bonking. Gettin' busy. Feeding the kitty. Knocking boots. Doing the horizontal hula. Making whoopee. Bit of the old in and out. Sexy time. Like, all the time. Shagging morning, noon, and night, if possible.

A house bereft of children doesn't have to mean a house bereft of fun. For some, it just means more time for cuddling in the morning, and a lot of extra hours during the rest of the day that can be whiled away engaging in the old slap and tickle. More time for rocking the casbah. More time doing the mattress mambo on Hump Day. Who needs a hobby when you can celebrate Humptoberbest every month, and have your own private Humpalooza? Who needs to travel, when you can Visit the Netherlands, or Park the Pink Plymouth in the Garage of Love? You get the picture. It's time for Happy Pants. And if the idea of having sex all day long seems a bit much, well, you can always lie back and think of England. And more euphemisms for laying some pipe.

IN PRAISE OF DOING NOTHING

Because it's true, maybe you feel like you have worked forever, either raising children full-time, or working at a part- or full-time job while also raising children (which is like having four jobs, honestly). So when you look back on these empty-nest years, sure, you'll remember the transition, the startling change, the searching, the celebrating . . . but you really want to be looking back on a person who got to finally freakin' relax.

You may have no desire whatsoever to climb mountains or read Dickens, and you really wish I would cut out all this overachiever crap. Haven't you done enough? Yes, yes you have. I hereby give you permission to do absolutely nothing. Get yourself a hammock. Or a La-Z-Boy, even. (I mean the recliner, not another person around the house who won't lift a finger.) Enjoy a succession of idle days and revel in your underachievement. If you've always been a manic type-A, with nineteen things on your plate at a time—like, for instance, a mother—then doing exactly nothing might be exactly what you need.

Learn to be a sloth, and without guilt. Wallow in languid inactivity. Daydream, lounge, and loaf. Stare at the ceiling. Nap. Dare to do nothing. After a few weeks of forced sluggishness, you'll know whether this is the life of which you've always dreamed, or whether you are about to jump out of your skin and it's time to get going. But no matter what you end up doing, don't forget to carve out some time for a little recharging every now and then.

A **PEARL OF WISDOM** FOR THE CHILD WHO HAS LEFT HOME

Seriously, are you getting drunk? Honey, sweetie. Sip. Alcohol is for sipping with charming friends while making witty remarks, and laughing in a tinkling and/or hearty fashion. If you end up bowing down to the porcelain throne—or whatever it is you kids are calling it these days—just know that you will be remembered forever that way. That is the picture your friends will have of you, ten, twenty years from now. You will go to a college reunion, and you'll be the guy they all remember heaving by the side of the road. On the other hand, vomiting could save you from alcohol poisoning, so there's that. Okay, just be careful, honey.

CURLING UP WITH A GOOD BOOK

Maybe you've never picked up any Thomas Hardy, because you think he seems too dreary and depressing. But you're wrong! Okay, fine, he's a little dreary and depressing. But he's dreary and depressing in the most delicious way! And tragic, to boot! Perhaps now is the ideal time to read *The Mayor of Casterbridge*. Or another delectable Victorian English classic, like *Middlemarch* (swoon!), *Jane Eyre* (sigh!), or *Little Dorrit* (a long, long, but wonderful book). If those suggestions are all too Brit-centric (sorry, I'm a sucker for bleak nineteenth-century English literature), you could read classics from around the world, hopping from one country to another. Pick a century, read the classics from that century from every continent. Or pick one author, and read everything he or she has ever written.

If you think you're just "not much of a reader," it could be simply that you're out of practice. Maybe you just didn't have that much time to read after you had your first child, and before you knew it, twenty-two years flew by and you realize now the only things you've managed to read for, like, ever are the back panels of cereal boxes and a few *Redbook* magazines at the dentist's office. You're not a shallow, ignorant, illiterate person, really, you're not. Some of us need books like we need oxygen and water, and some of us are fine with a few pages of the Calendar and Food sections of the online newspaper. But if it has been awhile since you picked up an actual book, well, you might want to give it another whack. Because honestly, there is really nothing like curling up on the sofa with a juicy book and getting lost in its pages for hours.

Sometimes you just have to carve out some time for reading. Maybe you still look at it as a "guilty pleasure," as if you're stealing chocolates. If you have all the best intentions but find you've developed the attention span of a cocker spaniel, perhaps you need a little hand-holding; a book group may be just the thing for you. A book group can be whatever you want it to be, really. It can be a group as small as you and a friend getting together at a regular time each month to talk about a book you both agreed to read. It can be a carefully chosen group of six, or twelve, or twenty. It can also be a not-so-carefully chosen free-for-all comprised of everyone you've ever met, or all the women you know, or a friendly group of couples. It can be a virtual book group with a select collection of Facebook friends, although that doesn't seem as cozy as meeting over tea and cakes.

The last book group of which I was a member (the *only* book group of which I've ever been a member) was a group of twelve women, which was the perfect size for this group, because we rotated houses each month. We rotated houses so that the burden of hosting wouldn't be on a single member. It meant that once a year each one of us would host the group for dinner. It was fortuitous that nearly every member happened to be a fantastic cook, in addition to being well read and opinionated. And honestly, the reading part was fun, but having a divine meal with a group of friends once a month was, between you and me, the best part.

College!
Not Just for the Kids

IF YOUR CHILD IS ABOUT TO SHIP OUT FOR COLLEGE, OR IS ALREADY there, chances are you recently spent a year or more perusing a multitude of college brochures and university Web sites with him and for him. Looking through stunning photos of verdant campuses, brick buildings dripping with ivy, intelligent-looking young people on rolling lawns, their noses in books. Many of us felt a vicarious thrill as we researched colleges for our offspring. And at times perhaps you heard a tiny voice inside, calling out in a wistful manner, "Hey! I want to live there!"

Alas, it may not be practical to attend college full-time at this moment in your life. Your spouse might take umbrage at the idea that you'll be "hanging out with your friends" during the Thanksgiving holiday, or that you'll "see him at spring break." But most towns have at least one community college. What in the world is stopping you from finally taking that Italian class you've been longing to take since before your first child was born? You probably have a general idea of what's on offer at various colleges around the country after poring over your child's college course list. So find the Web site of your local college, and look up the courses on offer.

For the adult extension–minded set, community colleges aren't just good for yoga and art classes, although they usually offer plenty of those. You could take some philosophy courses, or psychology, now that you're a person with a certain amount of experience under your belt. You could study poetry or learn sound engineering or filmmaking. You could learn jewelry making or print making or graphics. You could take a class just for fun and end up with a new skill that could lead to a new career. Or at least a new hobby.

There are art schools, music schools, and innumerable language courses available in most cities. If you live in a remote area, far away from anything resembling a community college, you'll find that most colleges offer online courses. Why not enlist a few friends and take some online classes together? Or better yet, advertise for a local instructor. For instance, let's say you can convince a few of your friends that you all need to learn French, or Spanish, or Chinese. Find a teacher in your town and arrange a class at your house, once or twice a week—so much more civilized than sitting in a stuffy room full of undergraduates or night-school denizens. You and your friends can make the specialty dishes of the various regions of whatever country whose language you're speaking. And enjoy some lovely indigenous wines or beers while you conjugate your verbs. You and your group can set goals. Plan a trip and set about learning everything you can about your intended destination. Gain some basic conversational skills and practice with each other between classes at the café or on a walk.

If they're amenable, get the spouses involved, so you'll have someone to practice with at home. Perhaps you and your live-in loved one are thinking about retiring to a foreign country? Why not pick a destination and start taking language classes together? There is nothing like hearing someone you love whisper *"Ti amo, il mio tesoro"* in your ear, especially if the person you've been living with for the past twentysomething years is more the type to crack a brewski and holler at the TV during a football game than serenade you on a gondola.

Scads of fascinating and informative lectures can be found online, like the TED talks, where you'll see musicians, poets, diplomats, authors, doctors, educators, artists, spiritual leaders, philosophers, architects, designers, and other interesting (and seemingly all well-spoken) people sharing their ideas, their philosophies, their thoughts about art. You can hear lectures by university professors at Harvard, Berkeley, Stanford, and other bastions of higher learning, on everything from particle physics to comparative literature. So if you just don't feel like getting into actual clothes and dragging yourself down to the local campus, you can immerse yourself in intellectual and creative stimulation of infinite variety, all from the privacy of your home. At your convenience. With a cup of coffee at 9 a.m., say, or a glass of wine at midnight.

Hang out at Yale for breakfast! Visit Princeton after dinner! It's not only a good way to find out if you might want to actually enroll in college again, it's also a great way to stuff your brain full of knowledge, which will at the very least make you a more captivating dinner companion.

Going back to school is not just a delightful way to fill your days; you'll be exposed to new ideas, thereby expanding your interests, and you're bound to meet new people, one or two of which might just add a lot of fun and inspiration or a sense of community and connection to your life. And it might as well be said now: Expanding your interests and keeping your brain active will keep dementia at bay. Too soon to be thinking about dementia? Um, not exactly. Now is the time you really want to step up that brain activity, so that you can be that erudite, fascinating, knowledgeable dinner companion for many, many years to come.

part 3

Stepping Out

13 Hello, Friends!

REMEMBER ALL THOSE PEOPLE YOU USED TO SEE, BEFORE YOUR children consumed every moment of your day? Remember those nice people you used to meet for coffee and lunch? The ones you could talk to and confide in? The ones who liked you even after you drank too much and said something dumb? Those people who would come for dinner and stay late, and you'd make each other laugh? Remember "friends"?

Now, remember all those years of sharing every detail of your children's lives with these friends? Not just your child's first steps, but every poo, tantrum, and adorable utterance? Remember regaling them with stories about your child's preschool years, and discussing the ins and outs of every playdate or sport and academic achievement? It may surprise you to know that most of your friends are very much looking forward to finding out what else might be on your mind.

If you still have any. If you inadvertently left a bunch of friends by the wayside while you were busy raising kids, maybe you want to revisit some of those relationships. Friends can be nice to have around, in case you've forgotten. Sure, you might be glad to be rid of a few of them—raising children often gives you the chance to divest yourself of certain persons you would really rather not have in your life anymore. Kids have a way of separating the men from the boys, so to speak. But there are a few friends you might have accidentally driven away, with a little too much talk of diapers, carpools, Little League, and the sleep habits of six-year-olds, or just from being chronically unavailable. Think about those few friends whose presence you've especially missed. The ones who left a small black hole where they used to be. The ones you think about wistfully, and wonder what they're up to. Those are the ones with whom you should reacquaint yourself, especially now that you no longer have to wrangle children's schedules in order to grab a simple cup of coffee.

If you no longer have their phone numbers or e-mail addresses, try looking for them on Facebook. If there's a whole group of friends with whom you've been out of touch, consider a reunion, which can be a great way to reconnect with a circle of old friends in one fell swoop. And if there are some members in a circle you have missed more than others, a group date also provides the opportunity to plan follow-up quality time with particular people.

On a different front, now that you're out of the fog of parenting and emerging from your self-imposed exile from the world of grown-ups, maybe you'd like to get to know some new people. But how do we do that, as grown-ups with old habits and set routines? The idea of looking for new friends sounds an awful lot like dating, a process that can feel daunting and/or horrible. You do need to put yourself out there, if you're going to connect with new people. But there are some ways of connecting that won't feel as desperate as others. For instance, let's say you have one or two friends. (Okay, let's just say you do. Okay, fine, but surely you have at least *one*.) You could start a book group with your friend. And you could ask her to invite one or two of her like-minded friends. And each of them could invite a few of their like-minded friends, and before you know it, you've got a dozen interesting people in a room talking about books.

Or maybe your favorite things about book groups are the food and wine consumed while talking about the books. So why not start a supper club, where you create a rotating dinner party with a group of people? A wine-tasting club is not only a great way to learn about wine, but also a wonderful way to expand your social group. There are rowing clubs, financial investment groups, hiking clubs—all ways to make new friends. Ask the friends you do have about clubs or groups they're a part of. Maybe you can let them know you're interested in joining, should the group be interested in adding a new member.

It could be that the friends you do have, you have by default. You all just sort of gravitated to one another because your kids were friends. Some of those relationships may fade, and for good reason. Now is the time for you to choose your own friends, without basing your choice on the fact that Maxwell has been little Dashiel's best friend since preschool, so you and Maxwell's mommy spent a lot of time drinking coffee together, even though you have very little

in common. In fact, she brags about Maxwell to an embarrassing degree plus makes you feel bad about your snack choices. Now Maxwell is off to Yale, and you really have no reason to ever see this woman again. Hooray!

On the other hand, you have a few true friends whose kids have also left home, and these friendships could be very valuable during this transition. Some of those old acquaintances may be going through a set of emotions similar to those you're experiencing in your empty nest. If you're not ready to plunge into a book group—or any other group activity, for that matter—these are the friends you can reach out to when you're feeling the rub of transitioning from full-time parent to full-time individual. Commiserate with each other. There may be only a few people who will understand what you're going through, and it's nice to have them around to vent with once in a while. But you can also help pull each other out of the occasional pits of wallowing and self-pity. Lean on them. But beware: Don't turn your sympathetic friends into a support group that just enables you to prolong your misery. You can all move on together. In fact, think about what an inspiration you can be to them. There's no better way to forget your own perceived troubles than to help someone else with theirs.

IN CASE YOU WEREN'T KIDDING
AND YOU REALLY DON'T HAVE ANY FRIENDS

It happens! It happens to a lot of people, I bet. You were really busy raising kids, maybe working a thousand hours a week, and then the kids left for college, and you started thinking about retiring, and you looked around and wondered, "Hey! Where is everybody?" Maybe you had a really high-powered job on top of being a mom, and you figured you were doing something pretty important, and your friends would be there when you finished making a bazillion bucks. But while you were really busy making a bazillion bucks and too busy to do stuff with your friends, those friends of yours had to continue living their lives, so they found other friends who enjoyed doing stuff with them. I know it's kind of awkward seeing them now, years later, but it happens.

Maybe you got divorced, and didn't realize that your ex-spouse was the one with all the friends when you were a couple. And you were busy getting your kids launched and out of the house, and now they're finally gone, but so are all those people you used to hang out with. It happens!

Friends are good to have around. But who do you spend the most time with? If you're married, it could be that you spend most of your time with your spouse, but if you're a divorced or a single parent, it might be that you spend most of the time with yourself. And you know, now that the kids are gone? Now might be the perfect time to spend some time figuring out who you are, and what you really want, and who it is you really want to be with (if you're in search of a partner) or if you want to be with anyone at all. If you've never spent much time on self-reflection, now might be a great time to delve a little deeper into your own issues. Life is really too short to not at least try to figure out some of this stuff, right? Like why we keep repeating the same patterns or reacting the same way to the same problems that keep cropping up, just because that's how we've always reacted to those problems. You could talk to a therapist or psychologist. You could go to a Zen retreat or learn meditation, or look into the various self-actualization programs out there.

Sure, some look at this sort of thing as so much navel-gazing, but I think the more we learn about ourselves, the better humans we'll ultimately be. Maybe you'll end up liking yourself a whole lot more. And becoming a more thoughtful, self-aware person might just inadvertently attract more friends than you ever thought you'd have.

A **PEARL OF WISDOM** FOR THE CHILD WHO HAS LEFT HOME

Don't be late! Please, do not be one of those "late people" who cannot ever be on time for anything. Don't leave your friends hanging out to dry because of your casual relationship with time. Show some respect for others, and be five minutes early. To everything.

Hey! The Kids Are Gone! It's Part-ay Time!

IT COULD BE THAT THE LAST EIGHTEEN-ODD YEARS HAVE CAUSED you to think of a "party" as something that entails either balloons or cake. Possibly a scary clown. Or perhaps chaperones, curfews, and rented tuxedos. But remember what having a party used to mean? In your newly child-and-teenager-free nest, you will have time to explore the various possibilities. In fact, how about starting with a grown-up cocktail party? You know, where adults convene in a room devoid of children, sip cocktails, and exchange witty banter. When was the last time you had one of those? I'm hoping not long ago. But I know far too many people who've been so caught up in getting their children successfully launched, they've pretty much forgotten how to do any adult entertaining. It really isn't all that complicated, it's fun, and it will snap you out of that crappy mood. You know: the crappy mood you've been in for way too long. Because you work too hard, and you're worried about your kid, who's about to go away to college or is already away at college. Or,

maybe you're just in a crappy mood because you haven't put on a cute party dress in a while.

If you're one of those fun fun fun people who cannot believe I'm even mentioning it, who has been throwing weekly cocktail parties since your children were toddlers, and for whom gin is mother's milk, well, please feel free to skip ahead. Mix yourself a drink while you're at it. Anyhoo, some of you have let yourselves get bogged down with work and life, and have forgotten that socializing with other people over a celebratory libation is one of the simple joys of life. You might think dress-up cocktail parties are only for other people, for sleek ladies and gents who work in the entertainment industry, or are on the boards of opera companies or international conglomerates. You think, sure, I have a few friends over for a bottle of wine every now and again, that's a cocktail party, right?

Well, I applaud your effort. But—disregarding the fact that "a glass of wine" cannot possibly ever be considered a cocktail, since a cocktail by my (and its original) definition must contain a splash of some flavor of bitters (but at the same time, not to say that "cocktails" are the only libation allowed at a cocktail party)—while getting together with a few pals over a glass of wine is a lovely thing to do, it's hardly a party. (Again, not to denigrate your lovely friends! And it's so true, isn't every moment spent with them a party, really?) In any event, a real cocktail party requires a certain amount of "dressing up," and perhaps a plate or two of finger foods to pass around to your guests. Now, just because I've said the word "guests" doesn't mean you need to invite a bunch of strangers over to the house. That's right, your best friends can, in fact, be the most special of special guests.

A cocktail party can be as simple or as elaborate as you want to make it. Serve one specialty cocktail for everyone, or set up a full bar and offer custom mixed cocktails. Hire a bartender, tend bar yourself, or tell everyone to help themselves. Of course you'll want to offer some nonalcoholic beverages and wine as an alternative for those who are not serious imbibers. The main thing is to have plenty of drinks on hand, of one sort or another—and enough tasty morsels to soak up whatever's on tap. Again, keep it simple or make it fancy, as you like. You can cover a linen-topped table with artfully assembled canapés, make swizzle sticks out of Himalayan salt–encrusted herb stems, scatter vases of stunningly arranged fresh flowers around the room. Or simply put out a few bowls of roasted nuts on the coffee table, maybe with some pretty cocktail napkins. The crucial thing is, you want to spend the evening enjoying your friends rather than being stuck in the kitchen or behind the bar, so make it easy on yourself by doing as much preparation ahead of time as you can.

If you haven't entertained for a while, don't fret about everything having to be "perfect" before you can have a party. Your house will never be "perfect." I hope your party has many flaws; this is what will make you more endearing and your party much more fun than a perfect party. Perfection is opening your home and hearth to people you like, and sharing your food and drink with friends in a relaxed atmosphere. If you really think your friends will be critically eyeing the chipped paint on your kitchen cabinets or judging you for mismatched powder room towels, then perhaps these people aren't very good friends.

I would be remiss if I didn't include a little something to help get your party under way, namely an easy recipe for something or other. Sometimes the simplest things can be the most memorable. A piece of bacon. Wrapped around a date. Broiled. It is a tiny taste of heaven. And even easier: my friend Maria's sweet and tasty bacon bites, full of sugary, bacon-y goodness. I have named them Sugar Pig. They are dangerously good, and really easy to make. Of course, you might have to go out and purchase bacon, which isn't a staple in everyone's house. But those who don't eat much bacon anymore will be stunned to see it on your table, and in such a highly edible and addictive form. There are dozens of recipes for this treat floating around the Internet (apparently it was very popular in suburbia a few decades ago), but my pal Maria gave me the real lowdown. The truth is, there are two ingredients.

Sugar Pig

1¼ cups firmly packed brown sugar
1 pound thinly sliced bacon

Preheat the oven to 350°F. Cover a baking sheet with aluminum foil or fit it with a rack. Put the brown sugar in a bowl. Cut your bacon slices in half and dredge each piece in the brown sugar. Lay the sugar-coated bacon pieces flat on the prepared baking sheet or the rack, without overlapping. Add a couple of twists to make them pretty, if you like. (Maria twists each bacon piece onto a bamboo skewer to shape them.) Bake until browned and crispy, about 15 to 20 minutes. (The sugar can burn easily, so check after 15 minutes.) Remove from the oven, and try to let them cool off a bit before the hordes start stuffing them down their gullets.

That's it. That's really it. Some recipes will tell you to add cinnamon, to which my friend Maria says "ick." And I have to say I agree with her in this case.

Traditionally, a cocktail party is meant to be an affair of two or three hours, and then everyone goes off somewhere else for dinner. But, depending on the group of friends you're inviting, you could call it a Cocktail and Light Supper Party—as long as you make enough hearty finger food that no one will feel as if they have to leave in order to get a proper meal. In addition to the nuts and tasty bacon snacks, you could put out a tray of sliced deli meats and cheeses for a do-it-yourself sandwich bar. Celebrate the sandwich. There is a good reason why the Earl of Sandwich had a convenience food named after him. What could be easier and more satisfying when you don't want a sit-down dinner? Offer a few choices of bread and buns, and relishes and grilled vegetables to go with the meats and cheeses. Set up an antipasti platter. Sliced peppers, carrots, and celery won't seem like rabbit food if you offer hearty dips and marinated olives alongside. The point is, parties are fun, and shouldn't be saved for special occasions. Be prepared! Always keep your pantry and your bar well stocked, so the idea of going into party mode is not a big deal, and so you are ready to throw a party at a moment's notice should the opportunity for a spontaneous gathering present itself.

MAY WE PLEASE
EAT SOME REAL GROWN-UP FOOD NOW?

One less mouth in the house to feed might mean one less finicky eater. If you haven't already banished your Pizza Fridays and Spaghetti Sundays child-friendly dining habits, now's your chance! Go ahead. If you've always catered to your children's limited palates, it's time to branch out into new and exciting food groups. It's also nice to be freed up from the routine of making three square meals a day. You can be a lot less regimented in your dining habits than when you had all the kids at home, and you perhaps felt obligated to cook your way into everyone's hearts. If your children always shied away from exotic fare, strong flavors, or any kind of greenery, why don't you try cooking up a mess of kale and some seared ahi tuna, and see what you've been missing all these years. And when your young adults come home on spring break, maybe they'll start flexing their taste buds too.

15 Sayonara, Mrs. Minivan

I'M TALKING TO YOU, O WEARER OF MOM JEANS. I KNOW, YOU WANT to be comfortable. Everyone wants to be *comfortable*. Well, I happen to believe that a beautiful woman (and all women are beautiful) can be just as comfortable in a pretty frock or a nice sweater set as they are in a pair of elastic-waist pants, a sweatshirt, and comfortable shoes. I'm not suggesting that you start wearing torturous six-inch stilettos around the house, and I certainly don't think women need to go back to the cavemen days of cinched girdles, lacquer hairspray, and sleeping in rollers and a hairnet. But my dears: The kids are gone. If not now, when? All that time you used to spend getting your kids off to school in the morning; making their breakfasts, lunches, and dinners; driving them hither and thither to music classes and the mall; well, that's a lot of extra time that is now at your disposal for pulling yourself together. Not because you're looking particularly awful, but because it's *fun*.

Honestly, when was the last time you played dress-up? You don't need an excuse, like going out to dinner or to a party. Make your own home-cooked dinner into a party—put a few candles on the table and doll yourself up, just because it feels good. Or *do* give yourself a reason to go out, and get really dressed up.

But we may find, at this post–Utilitarian Mom style juncture, that we don't really know what it means to dress up anymore. Or what we want it to mean, or how it should look and feel. Sometimes when we reach a "certain age," suddenly we have no idea of what we're supposed to look like. Surely you have a vague notion that you shouldn't be dressing like a twenty-year-old anymore, but you're not ready to dress like your mother, either. So you've been playing it pretty safe. Sweatpants and jeans. Perhaps a pale pastel cardigan. A pressed pair of khakis when you're really going all out. I don't want to dissuade you from a life of khaki and comfort, if you've really found your "uniform" and know that it makes you happy. But fashion can be so much fun, and it can be a wonderfully creative way to express ourselves.

"But I haven't bought any new clothes in ages!" you say. "I have nothing to wear!" Actually, you do. You have a closetful of clothes. But you tend to put on the same old comfy sweats or favorite jeans and T-shirts every day, and you haven't really looked at most of the clothing in your closet for a long, long time. A lot of the clothes hanging there are just waiting to be looked at again, and possibly repurposed. Take a look at your old outfits in a new way. Even if you don't sew, you can imagine. Imagine that old jacket without shoulder pads. Imagine the bottom half of that dress as a chic skirt.

(The top half never fit very well anyway.) Imagine that skirt (which was always too short) with an extra panel sewn across the bottom. Now, doesn't that look better? And you can take the extra panel from that old-new dress that you got ten years ago and only wore twice. If you are absolutely hopeless with a needle and thread, enlist a nice friend with a sewing machine. It's also easy to find yourself a local tailor; support a small business in your community *and* end up with a new wardrobe!

Dressing for the empty nest is also a matter of reimagining yourself. You can be your own blank canvas. A dress or a skirt can be just as comfy as an old pair of sweats, it just gives the impression that you care a tiny bit more. So get yourself a little black dress, if you don't already have one. Find yourself a slimming pencil skirt and a cashmere cardigan, which isn't as expensive as it sounds, and can often be found in a decent thrift store. Get one that fits well, not one that looks as if your large Polish grandmother wore it to vespers. Get yourself some red lipstick! Please. Really, it'll look great. Whoever told you that red lipstick is "aging" just wanted you to look boring. They probably wanted all the red lipstick for themselves. I bet they also told you that you should never wear red lipstick during the day. Who are these people, and why do women listen to them? Buy a lovely red lipstick, and put it on in the daytime, in the evening, in the wee hours of the morning. Even if I can't get you out of your comfy old jeans, your red lipstick will pull together your whole look. (Especially if you tie your hair back and wear a clean oxford shirt or lint-free cashmere pullover. Hello, Grace Kelly!)

There may come a time when you want to let your grey hair grow down to your knees, or perhaps shave it off completely. There may come a time when you see yourself wearing nothing but a muumuu, a hoodie, and a pair of flip-flops every day, as you putter around the house, happy to be puttering around anywhere at your age. But I'm guessing you may not have reached that point quite yet. I bet you still have a few new hairdos to try before you throw in the towel. If you've been tying your hair back in the same Mom Ponytail for the last twenty years, maybe it's time to let it down. Dye it bright red. Chop it off, or grow it down your back. Pile it up on top of your head and pretend you're an Italian movie star. Just try something a little different, and shake things up a little.

Comfort is important, but so is style. And I think it's possible to have both. If you've never been all that interested in "fashion," you can still develop some "style." Style does not require a passion for (or being a slave to) fashion, and just because you're "fashion-able" it doesn't necessarily mean you've got style. It's not impossible to develop a style of your own, even over a certain age. Have fun! Experiment. And I can't stress enough, it doesn't hurt to invest in a bold red lipstick.

Your Fashion Inspiration

*Tavi Gevinson, Anna Dello Russo, Lynn Yaeger,
and That Lady You Saw Buying Peaches
at the Farmers' Market*

SO, WHAT IF YOU REALLY WOULD LIKE TO SHAKE THINGS UP IN
your humdrum old closet, but you have no idea where to start. In
fact, you may never have been much of a fashion maven. Indeed
you'd prefer it if there was a simple pill you could take that would
render you dressed for the day. But since no such pill has yet been
invented, you choose from a standard collection of pull-on clothing in a tasteful, safe palette. Outfits that *match*. Ensembles that can
be donned without thinking too hard. You will be dressed, yes. But
where is the fun in just being dressed? Perhaps you really don't have
a stylish bone in your body. But if you enjoy dressing up, even just
a tiny bit, then let yourself be open to inspiration. Which can be
found pretty much everywhere.

I started reading Tavi Gevinson's *Style Rookie* blog a few years
ago—when Tavi was about thirteen years old. I think she started
the blog when she was twelve. Twelve! So at this point, she is an old
hand in the world of fashion, has been interviewed in countless

magazines, and gets swag sent to her regularly from Miu Miu and Proenza Schouler. But what she does with the swag is put it together—in an inspired and inventive way—with thrift store finds and stuff she has in her regular teenage wardrobe. Her style is not for everyone, but it's full of joy and a loopy creativity. And sometimes her style choices are so unusual they will make you want to try dressing up in combinations that heretofore would have seemed ridiculous. It's true, if you attempt to approximate Tavi's stylings on any given day, you might end up looking like a crazy bag lady. After all, she's a teenager, and her particular fashion choices look absolutely perfect on her. But she might inspire you to break out of your boring old mind-set when it comes to sartorial style.

Same with Anna Dello Russo, the Italian editor of *Vogue* Japan. The woman who has two apartments in Milan, one devoted entirely to her clothing. It's an apartment-size closet. Dang! Ain't it the life. She owns, like, four thousand pairs of shoes. That's probably a low estimate. That kind of conspicuous consumption would normally make me grind my teeth in horror, but after all, it is her job. And after seeing an interview with her, I couldn't help but be tickled and charmed, she is so full of love and enthusiasm for fashion.

Not for her the austere black dress or perfectly chic Chanel suit that most fashion editors call their uniform. She doesn't wear the requisite black to the runway shows because she finds it "depressing." Ms. Dello Russo looks as if she could float down any runway, if that runway was full of smiling models wearing tea cozies and giant apples on their heads and green faux monkey fur on their backs. She recommends turning on music and dancing "naked by candlelight" before you get dressed for the evening. This, she believes, will help you decide what to wear, because the spirit of your outfit will call out to you. It seems to me like a perfectly sensible way to choose an ensemble.

Ms. Dello Russo is obviously head over heels with fashion and style, and she clearly has a sense of humor about it. And if you're going to be in charge of *Vogue* Japan, you really had better have one, considering the culture of street fashion and the Harajuku Girls who roam the streets in their Goth-Lolita garb. Seriously, if you want to feel like a boring old suburban matron, have a look at some Tokyo street fashion. It might just light a tiny fire under your beige khaki bottom, and make you want to edge a little bit farther out on a fashion limb.

But perhaps my favorite role model for style, just for sheer cheek and sense of fun, is copper-bobbed fashion writer Lynn Yaeger. Growing up with a round physique and paper-white skin in an era when tan and thin was in, she turned what much of the world around her surely considered liabilities into assets, turning herself out as a woman resembling, to me, a Victorian Kewpie doll, one who might have been photographed by Bressai in a Parisian brothel in 1925. She is over fifty, and walks around New York with her signature rouge-dotted cheeks and flaming bob, sporting petticoats, furs, and ribbons. I am smitten by her charm and self-confidence and utter whimsy, and aspire to that kind of fashion fearlessness when I grow up.

Okay, I have given you three of my own personal fashion inspirations, all of whom, admittedly, have a heightened fashion sense that some might describe as "kooky." My wonderful editor suggested that I instead mention a bunch of classy dames of a certain age who are gorgeous and stylish—but slightly more toned down—such as Jamie Lee Curtis, Michelle Obama, and Michelle Pfeiffer. Jamie Lee Curtis is a lovely example of mature stylishness, and I enjoy Mrs. Obama's well-coordinated ensembles, but it is constitutionally impossible for me to put them down as personal fashion inspirations. (Although I do love Ms. Curtis's chic silver haircut.) Also, I am sad to say, Michelle Pfeiffer has had too many startling surgical adjustments done on her face for me to put her on my list. Sorry! Yes, it's true that my aforementioned Women of Fashion could be considered by many of you as far too silly to be true fashion icons. But the reason I share them as inspirations of style is to demonstrate how much fun it can be when you stretch yourself a little, fashion-wise, when you flex a few rarely used style muscles.

You may not want to stretch yourself quite that far; in fact, you might prefer needles in your eyes to being seen in public wearing a mismatched pair of socks and a bird's nest on your head. But it's possible to find fashion and style inspiration everywhere. And I figure, if Bjork can wear a stuffed swan with a tulle and feather skirt, then we might be surprised to find that we're brave enough to try wearing a hat or a pair of bright red boots, or dig deep into our closets and invent an interesting ensemble completely different from one of our usual staid combinations. A matching ensemble won't offend anyone, but perfection just isn't very interesting. And don't forget: You no longer have your kid at home looking sideways at what you're wearing.

To find your own inspirations and style heroes, start by flipping through a few magazines. Rather than looking at whole ensembles or finding new reasons to feel bad about your thighs, look for new pieces to add to your puzzle. A bright shoe color, a messy upsweep of hair, a look you've never tried. Start putting together a picture of your reimagined self. If you have a free hour in the house alone, that's the time to mix lipstick colors, to try out a Brigitte Bardot bouffant, to see what the heck a dramatic eyeliner might look like, just for fun. If it looks absolutely ridiculous, then no one's the wiser. (Except perhaps the UPS man, who happened to drop a package off mid-bronzing cream and orange lipstick.)

It's not about slavishly copying exactly what you see on the pages of *Vogue* or *W*; fashion photos should merely be a jumping-off point. Half the time I look through fashion magazines, I'm swooning over the frocks; the other half I am incredulous that there can be that many hideous outfits all in one place. Obviously, that burlap bubble dress might not look quite the same way on you as it does on that nineteen-year-old wafer-thin model. Models have a way of making ridiculous clothing look kinda kicky. But sometimes a color combination or a silhouette will inspire an idea, or prompt a desire to try a little something new.

If your kids have grown up and left home, and you are inching toward that "certain age" feeling mopey and matronly and less than beautiful, then you need to expand your definition of beauty. You will never have your twenty-year-old body back, but you can learn to adore the one you've got now. If you need to get that body in better shape for your health, then do that; but a few extra pounds and a smattering of laugh lines shouldn't cause you to throw in the towel. Style is ageless.

Take a walk. Be inspired by your friends. Be inspired by that interesting woman you saw picking over the peaches at the farmers' market. The one dressed in a simple shirtdress and flats, with choppy, bright crayon-red hair. The one with the dark purple lipstick, who seemed so gorgeously comfortable in her less-than-stick-thin body. You may have a friend you've never really thought of as "fashionable," but she's got a good sense of how she puts herself together. She somehow ends up being captivating, even though she would never be considered a great beauty. If you're absolutely mystified over this whole "How in the world am I supposed to dress at my age?" thing, maybe your friend can give you a few tips. Style has very little to do with clothes, and much more to do with grace, self-confidence, and a sturdy sense of humor. And we could do worse than spending the rest of our lives cultivating those particular qualities, right? Especially the sense of humor. You will definitely need as much of that as possible.

17 Life Is Too Short for Sweatpants

A Short, Sartorial Guide for the Stay-at-Home, Freelance, or Retired Gentleman*

WHETHER YOU HAVE BEEN A STAY-AT-HOME DAD, A FREELANCER working from home, or are retiring as your last child goes off to college, the lady of the house has got a few helpful hints for you.

Those baggy gray sweatpants looked absolutely adorable on you when you were in your twenties and thirties. But you're getting, um, how do I say this? Older? Older and wiser. And full of gravitas, I might add. Perhaps a pair of smart trousers would do more for your look, at this moment in your life. Being silver-haired and dignified doesn't mean you have to go all stuffy and starched-shirt on us. But as we age, wearing something a little more pulled together really helps put a little giddyap in the step. A smart ensemble can do more for depression and a case of ennui than a case of Prozac. And trust me, the girls really go for a man of style—if by "the girls," you

---

*A useful chapter that may need to be brought to the attention of certain people, perhaps by leaving the book casually lying around, open to this page. (Place on the back of the toilet or on top of the television remote for best results.)

understand it to mean "your wife of twenty-odd years who hears you in the bathroom every morning."

You may think that men's fashion is hideous, or ridiculous, and a sport only for the young and gay. But here's a thought, big boy: "Style" has very little to do with "fashion." You can be a snappy dresser and a man of style without ever opening a *Gentlemen's Quarterly* or getting fitted on Saville Row. It's a matter of deciding who you want to be in this new stage of your life.

"But wait," you say, "I know who I want to be. I want to be the guy who shuffles around the house in a pair of baggy sweatpants! The kids are gone, for god's sake! Can't I wear a pair of goddamn sweatpants and an old white T-shirt for days on end? Can't I be comfortable? And what's this obsession over teeth brushing and shaving *every single day*? Leave me alone!"

Well, the thing is, you don't really want to be alone. Do you? Because the thing is, as we get older and become more distinguished and full of that old gravitas, a little more time and care must be spent pulling oneself together. Ask any woman; what worked quite well when we were in our twenties and thirties doesn't necessarily work to our advantage in our forties, fifties, and beyond. That cute chick you married might have worn a baseball cap and miniskirt twenty years ago; but do you really want her to be donning skinny leggings and that baby-doll micromini when she's heading into her seventies? Or what if she slunk about in a baggy old pair of sweatpants and gym socks every day, because it's just "more comfortable?" (Et tu, ladies?) You can love each other to death, but when someone looks as if he or she has as much pride in their appearance as, say, our neighbor who washes his car in his Red Sox boxers, then you just start wondering.

Sure, you dress up once in a while, when you go out to a party, or out to a restaurant. But when you come home, you can't wait to get out of that monkey suit and get comfortable, right? Of course, I understand the need to be "comfortable" when you're at home. But what if you and your spouse are both at home together a lot? Like, all the time. Seriously. Every day, now that the kids have left. And if you only get dressed up when you're forced to leave the house, then she's the lucky girl who gets to see you in your worn-out baggy ol' sweatpants. Every day.

If you are this kind of guy, basically alternating between sweat-pants and jeans and back to sweatpants because you have no idea what else to wear, then I would suggest this: Look to the classics. Cary Grant was always well turned out, even as an elderly gentleman. One can't imagine Cary Grant in anything but a nice open-collared oxford shirt tucked into a pair of gabardine trousers, casually topped by a navy blue jacket. Unless he was wearing a tuxedo. Or a smoking jacket. And why not revive the smoking jacket? The point is, if

you're the kind of gent who needs simplicity, you can still find a great look for this next chapter of your life; you just need to find a simple solution to your post-kid stylish uniform. This uniform could be as old-school simple as the oxford shirt, gabardine trousers, and polished loafers (no socks). Or, if you're craving a changeup, something more whimsical: say, a houndstooth suit and bow tie, with saddle oxfords. Or a mid-century skinny black suit and skinny tie. Or a comfy tweed, with a vest and boutonniere. And yes, even jeans and a pullover, as long as everything fits well. If you're on a budget, you can pull some mean ensembles together with a few thrift-store sprees. If you've got a little extra scratch, start collecting some quality pieces and put together a real wardrobe. Try getting creative with your facial hair! Perhaps it's time to find out how you really look with a scruffy beard or goatee.

The point is: Take pride in your appearance. Stand up a little straighter. Walk with purpose. Clothes do not make the man, but they do make the man look a whole lot cuter (along with the grooming and the teeth brushing). And it's not just about superficial appearance. Your mental health will improve. People will remark upon your appearance, which will make you feel even better about yourself. You won't look as if you've given up on life. And seriously, aren't you a tiny bit tired of dressing like a perennial post-adolescent slacker who's on his way to a pickup basketball game?

And get out of the house once in a while. It's good for you to get out into the world, and it's good for your significant other for you to get out in the world. If you're always at home, you can never be missed. And when you come home after being out in the world, you will have new things to talk about. You will have seen a few things. You will have gotten a little fresh air, and so will your relationship. The point is, if you've always been sort of a stay-at-home person, you might want to find a few Interests outside the house. Please. Please do this. For your own sake, and for the sake of the person you live with.

And when you do, you'll have a new reason to put on a smart pair of trousers and a crisp, well-fitted shirt. You'll feel like a million bucks, and the person you come home to will so appreciate the effort.

A **PEARL OF WISDOM** FOR THE CHILD WHO HAS LEFT HOME

Work on your penmanship. I know it seems like a useless thing to you right now, but it's becoming a lost art. So practice your handwriting every now and then. Why? Because it's always a good thing to know how to write a legible love letter. If not for yourself, for others. It's a skill. And someday you might want to write a real letter to someone. Just because you can. Keep some nice notepaper around, with some envelopes. And get a sheet of stamps, just in case.

You.
Off the Couch.
Now.

SPEAKING OF EXERCISE (OKAY FINE, WE WEREN'T TALKING ABOUT exercise, but now I'm afraid we must), it's time you started getting some. We are at an age when we need to, ugh, exercise. Yes, it's true. Our bodies, apparently, will not exercise themselves while we sleep. I know, after raising a couple of children, you may feel you've done enough. You're perfectly comfortable doing nothing but keeping the house picked up, reading the paper from cover to cover, and watching your "shows." You may even consider yourself active. After all, you walk to the post office and the corner store. You have once or twice, anyway. You even walk to your local farmers' market every now and then. And certainly you walk to your car, at least a few times a day.

I know how easy it is to find a million things you'd rather be doing than exercising. But aren't we a little young to be behaving like retired people? And your body *will* take an early retirement if you don't start moving it on a much more regular basis.

So if you aren't already one of those paragons of health who has built some sort of invigorating exercise program into your life, then it really is time you did something about it. And taking on a few physical challenges can be a truly rewarding way to pull yourself out of the empty-nest doldrums, should you be experiencing such a thing (and I'm guessing you've had at least a tinge or two, since you are reading this book).

Why not think big and start training for a marathon (or—thinking big but being realistic—a half marathon)! A lot of perfectly ordinary mortals seem to be doing it these days. If you don't feel that you're up for a group event that requires you to run for a ridiculously long period of time—or if you shudder at the thought of running anywhere, for any length of time—then create your own marathon. You can even, without guilt, walk, don't run. Find a destination, say, one to five miles from your house. Then plan an outing that will get you from point A to point B. Enlist a few friends. Make a party of it. Sure, you could become a mall walker, but why not explore a part of your town you've never explored before? Once a week you could walk to any given three- to five-mile destination. For instance, I live seven miles from the beach. The Pacific Ocean! I have ridden my bike along the bike paths and the path along the L.A. River. But I have never actually walked those seven miles to the beach. For heaven's sake, what am I waiting for?

Look at a map (Google Maps are so much fun) and find a destination near your house. Start out with one mile, if you want to ease into it. Change your destination on a weekly basis. You could start your own Five-Mile Club! Or Two-Mile Club. Or Seven-Mile Club. You'll discover restaurants, parks, and shops you never knew existed. Find a friend and walk to your destination, picking a place to eat on the way back. Or meet a group of friends when you arrive, and get a ride home from them.

Okay, maybe running is too painful, and walking's too boring. What about taking up dancing? If you haven't seen the inside of a ballet classroom since your tutu fell down during the recital at Miss Darlene's Dance Studio thirty-five years ago, you don't know what you're missing. And it shouldn't be too difficult to find adult ballet classes—not to mention jazz, Latin jazz, Afro-jazz, and so on. It's not only a challenging workout, it'll do wonders for your posture, balance, and grace. Or maybe you could talk your significant other into taking a ballroom or swing dancing class? Once you learn how to dance together, you can start looking for venues around town, where you can practice your newfound moves. Which means evenings together that don't involve sitting in front of a TV screen! Date nights that entail more than just going out to eat!

If you are still on the floor laughing at the idea of your spouse taking a dance class with you—well, why not ask? Perhaps your partner has no sense of rhythm and is intimidated by the idea. You could both be intimidated by the idea. But that's the point of a challenge. A dance class might challenge both of your assumptions about what you're each capable of doing. It also might challenge your assumptions about the kind of people who take dance classes, and what you expect from taking a dance class. The goal need not be an audition for *Dancing with the Stars* at the end of the course. It's just something fun to do. Together. Okay, fine, stop laughing. Maybe you will never convince your mate to slip into a pair of Capezios and take to the dance floor. But if there's a latent Ginger Rogers simmering inside of you, maybe you can find a friend who'll join you in a few lessons. You need to start moving more, you really do. So you might as well find some fun ways to do it.

If you need to trick yourself into exercising, as I often must do, make a movie date with a pal, and plan to walk there. You'll feel so virtuous having walked the two miles to the theater, and your reward will be getting to sit with your friend in front of the big screen with a bag of popcorn. And then you can walk home, adding another couple of miles to your daily constitutional. Or ask your spouse to come pick you up, and make a date out of the evening.

You don't have to rush home to feed children, remember? Nor do you need to get to sleep early because you have to attend that School Booster Club meeting first thing in the morning. Whoa. You know what that means? You won't ever have to see that crazy group of Tiger Moms ever again. Doesn't that put a little spring in your step?

JOJO THE DOG-FACED BOY, THE SWORD SWALLOWER, AND YOU

If walking down to your local coffeehouse a couple of times a week just isn't giving you the aerobic kick you need, then it really is time to find something that will inspire you to move that derriere off the sofa. Join the circus! Or if you think that at your age, life in the circus might not be as comfortable as one would hope, at least take a trapeze class. What I mean is: Finding some sort of vigorous activity that you love to do is half the battle. A friend of mine learned the art of the trapeze in her forties, worked her butt off, and loved every minute of it. It's not as if she ended up actually joining the circus, but she gained strength and self-confidence while simultaneously fulfilling her own circus-girl fantasy. And it did wonders for her upper arms. Reason enough?

19 Feathering Your Empty Nest

SO YOU'VE LAUNCHED YOUR CHILD INTO THE POST-HIGH-SCHOOL world. And here you are, getting used to living in a very empty nest. Is it time to sit forlornly in his old bedroom, reminiscing over the old class photos, the awards, the series of self-portraits he did in kindergarten, only rising to take in a small bit of nourishment? And, perhaps, dust the Little League trophies? No. It's time to redecorate! Preferably before he comes home for Thanksgiving. It's time to find several empty cardboard boxes and bring them into the bedroom that formerly housed your child.

Minutiae first: Invest in a few storage boxes with lids. That way you can save the good stuff for your child to go through at a later date. Use your other boxes and old grocery bags for garbage and recycling.

Be ruthless. Sure, save the cheap plastic trophies he received for merely showing up to whatever sporting event he joined, or art competition he entered. But do you really need to hang on to the picture frame decorated with fifteen-year-old Cheerios? Will he really miss the pirate ship fashioned from a shoebox and chopsticks? Will he truly wonder what happened to the bridge made of tongue depressors and rubber bands? The adorable Space Rabbit pictures he crayoned in first grade (during his heady Space Rabbit phase) are looking a little curly around the edges. If you must save them, perhaps it would do them good to be flattened inside a portfolio, or a heavy book.

If you've been thinking about downsizing, you don't necessarily have to move out in order to declutter, reorganize, and cut back on the amount of stuff you've got. Obviously, moving to a smaller house or apartment will force the issue and accelerate the process; but if you're not quite ready to take that big a leap, simply pretend you're planning a move, and start divesting. You have no idea how satisfying it will be to actually *throw away* three entire shelves' worth of VHS tapes and a haphazard collection of single socks and old baseball cleats.

If you raised your children in this house or apartment, it's possible that you could be a little overwhelmed by the prospect of a deep cleaning. Even a reasonably small house or apartment can end up being a receptacle for what seems like a lifetime of stuff. Where to begin? Well, why not start with one room, then move on to the next! From room, to room. You can do it. Because some will be in better shape than others, and the easy ones will make you feel less daunted by the whole project.

So let's start with your child's bedroom. Too soon? Possibly you were planning on leaving everything as is and turning it into some kind of shrine? Maybe you were just going to start calling it the "guest bedroom," thereby keeping it open for all of your child's holiday visits? Which is a fine thing, if you've got so many rooms in your house that you can keep one unused for most of the year without anyone noticing. But there are a few other alternatives.

Why not turn your child's room into your very own walk-in closet? Come on, don't tell me you don't need some extra closet space. Don't tell me you haven't ever longed for one of those elegant, ladylike dressing rooms. Something with a mirrored vanity, silver brushes, and powder puffs displayed across the top, a tufted satin stool tucked underneath. A room the color of pink washed silk, with gold bamboo stalks painted on the wall. A divan. But mostly, a closet with room for dresses and coats and your Imelda-size collection of shoes. The dresses, coats, and shoes you haven't worn all these years because you've been too busy driving carpools and carting your busy children hither and thither while wearing baggy sweatpants. If you don't fit into those clothes anymore, you'll now have room for some *new* dresses, coats, and shoes. Gardeners often suggest that one should never buy new seedlings before the holes have been dug. Cleaning out your child's room is the equivalent of digging those holes. So start digging!

Think about the many creative projects you've never had the room to try. Sure, you set up an easel in the corner of the patio one weekend a few years ago. But you've never had the room to really spread out and make a nice mess—until now. Transform your child's room into a crafts room, art studio, or sewing room. You can keep the bed in there as a place to lie down and daydream while you're waiting for paint or glue to dry. Replace those yellowing indie-rock posters dotting the walls with your own creations.

Move your TV from its place of honor in the middle of the living room (where it blocks the fireplace) and create your own cozy media center. Add some pillows to the bed for a place to snuggle when it's just the two of you (or replace it with a sofa bed); add a few comfortable chairs for when you have friends over. It's a parlor! A media parlor. Paint the walls a dark but welcoming color, hang a few vintage movie posters, and install a low coffee table for snacks. Movie night, anyone?

If you move that old stationary bike in there, you might find you use it more often. And in your media parlor/exercise room, you can pop a pilates DVD into the machine and sweat in the privacy of your own home. Is there room for a ballet barre? Have you always wanted a yoga room? Or maybe a music room, with a piano you can practice privately?

Your child leaving the nest might also give you the possibility of making a bit of extra cash with that extra room. Get a boarder, or a foreign exchange student. Better yet, place your extra room on a site that deals with short-term rentals. You could end up hosting a string of interesting European travelers and people coming to town on business, and you might make enough cash to finally take that vacation you thought you'd never get since spending your nest egg on SAT tutors and college tours.

Once your "spare" room has been reconfigured and lightened up, the whole house will feel lighter. Move into the living room, the dining room, whatever rooms are left. Look around each one of those rooms. When was the last time you really got in there and got rid of stuff? Are there still tiny cars hiding in drawers, a collection of dolls lying around on shelves, many of them missing arms and hair? Are there three sets of Monopoly tucked under the sideboard, all of them missing top hats and Go to Jail cards? Those small plastic Hungry Hippos balls may be turning up for years to come, but you can certainly make a dent in your living space. If you know your kids are going to want to break out the Connect Four and the Scattergories when the families all get together over the holidays, then make a special spot for those games both children and adults will enjoy. And if you have been saving every toy you ever bought for your children since before they were born, and your garage and attic are filled to the rafters with stuffed animals, plastic cars, and Sit 'n Spins, you should seriously think about having a garage sale. Or better yet, donating the collection to charity, or a local preschool. If your kids really want to keep their childhood toys, make a box up for each child, containing the things you know they loved best. And give away the rest of it. No one will ever be the wiser.

While you're going through old books and games and throwing out assorted junk, have a cold, hard look around your living space. (Maybe have a cold, hard drink, while you're at it. This work is grueling!) Is this where you want to be when you retire? Is this where you want to live forever? If the answer to those questions turns out to be no, you might find your spring cleaning becoming a little more ruthless.

20 Your Next Chapter

Downsizing Your Life

YOU PROVIDED THE KIDS WITH A NICE ROOF OVER THEIR HEADS; a happy neighborhood where they could ride their bikes and occasionally knock on a neighbor's door; a good, local school; and all the support they needed to get through those school years. Okay, maybe it was a small apartment, a street full of traffic, and your neighborhood was less Mayberry and more *8 Mile*. But you did your best. And now they're off: embarking on careers, living their lives—and in some cases, actually doing their own laundry and grocery shopping and paying their own rent.

It's time for that next step—that next step for you, I mean. Are you really thinking of keeping the house forever so the children will have a place to bring their children, and you can watch the clan play touch football on the lawn, like Rose Kennedy? At what point do you get to decide whether it's what you want? I mean, sure, if I lived on the Kennedy compound in Hyannis Port then I'd probably want to stay too, but let's just say you don't. Let's just say you occasionally ponder paying the mortgage forever on a two- or three-bedroom house that may or may not need the foundation fixed, the cracks in the wall patched every other year, and the peeling paint repainted. Paying a mortgage. Every month. Until you are seventy-five. On a house that could have used a good kitchen remodel about ten years ago, and may not get one in the foreseeable future. This is my life? Really? Forever? Just so the kids can come home and rifle through the fridge and put more water rings on the coffee table?

Or maybe you've been living in a colossal McMansion, with enough square footage to house a small village of people. Your kids are gone, having fled the suburban lifestyle in which they were raised. There are just two of you in five-thousand-plus square feet of gleaming Corian countertops, dazzling hardwood flooring, and roomfuls of sofas, armoires, and flat-screen televisions. Not counting the housekeeper who has to come three times a week just to keep all those bedrooms dusted and bathrooms scoured. Or the team of gardeners who have to mow and trim that water-thirsty landscaping. Your four-car garage (heated to a toasty seventy-eight degrees, just like every square inch of your mostly unused mansion) houses the requisite midlife sports car, the minivan, and the unwieldy SUV. The rest of it is full to the brim with rarely used sporting equipment, Jet Skis, dirt bikes, and hockey, baseball, and soccer paraphernalia. And a full-size trampoline, leaning on its side, against the wall. Everything necessary for pool-time fun is stored in your fully furnished pool house, for the pool that's heated year-round ("Just in case!") even though it's only used one or two months of the year.

This isn't just the super-rich consuming such a vast amount of resources; it's hundreds of thousands of upper-middle-class families, whose collective carbon footprint makes Godzilla's look rather petite. If you're not yet ready to downsize, at least consider turning off a few of those water heaters and unplugging the extra fridge in the rumpus room. Solar panels on the roof would be a splendid idea. But if the idea of relentless upkeep and unending expense to keep your domestic behemoth fed and cared for is starting to feel like a giant ball and chain around your neck, maybe it's time to consider trading down.

Concerned that the Joneses will think you've come down in the world? Well, guess what? The Joneses have got a monthly nut that is just about killing them, they've got one kid in rehab and another with student loans to pay off for the next hundred years, and they haven't the foggiest idea how they're going to pay their ballooning home equity line of credit this month. They had to let their gardener go, for god's sake. The Joneses do not give a flying crap whether you open a nudist colony next door or relocate to an igloo in the Yukon.

So maybe you've secretly pondered the idea of moving to a simple adobe somewhere in the desert. Or maybe a small apartment in a big city sounds more appealing; a tidy place requiring little upkeep. A pied-à-terre you can use as your hub when you want to take off traveling on a whim. Maybe you've imagined building your own "dream house." Now might be the perfect time to do it. You could sell your monster-manor, buy a piece of rustic land, and build from scratch. Which doesn't necessarily mean you have to sign up for a decade-long construction nightmare; you could erect a yurt, or a modern prefab, either of which can be installed in a matter of days or weeks.

There are many options to living the sometimes barely affordable American Dream. So many options to "keeping house," keeping a house up, and spending your golden years entrenched in property taxes, roof repairs, and lawn maintenance. Whether you polish your own furniture or watch someone else polish your furniture, you still might want to consider whether the amount of furniture you have is really necessary for your needs at this time in your life. On the other hand, your house might be your haven, your oasis, your pride and joy. You love to spend time in it with friends, your family, and all by yourself; you can't imagine your life without your house and garden, and you're not leaving. Ever. Unless it's feetfirst. There is a lot to be said for maintaining a warm and inviting haven to which friends and family are encouraged to flock. And if you derive personal enjoyment and satisfaction from your house, and it gives you a happy feeling whenever you look around, then the upkeep and maintenance will be worth it. And for many of us, there's no place like home.

21 Running Away from Home

When Downsizing Just Isn't Enough

MAYBE THE IDEA OF TRAVELING AROUND THE GLOBE AND BEING a tourist in foreign ports sounds great, but . . . a part of you wants more than just the two-week trip to Italy every five years.

Maybe a big part. In fact, a rather giant part of your being longs for foreign shores. This is one of those big, potentially life-changing moments: Think. Have you ever considered retiring in a foreign country once the children have flown the coop?

You could love the idea, but be assailed by doubt, or at the very least, intimidated. Perhaps you've dreamed about it for so long you can only imagine dreaming about it, not actually doing it. But take it one step at a time. There are shelves full of books and hundreds of online sites that can get you started. The first one I ever came across is called *The Grown-Up's Guide to Running Away from Home*, by Rosanne Knorr. Such an enticing title. Because who hasn't ever dreamed of running away from home?

Of course, it's a giant step from a short holiday to becoming an expat. You may feel anxious about permanently pulling up stakes.

You may not want to completely give up your home country, and if you speak no languages other than English, you may feel disconcerted by the idea of having to struggle to get your point across. But you may be surprised to know how many American and other English-speaking expatriates have retired abroad. Of course you'll want to immerse yourself in the culture and language of your newfound country, but it's nice to know that if you really need to blow off some steam in your native tongue, you'll be able to find fellow travelers with whom you can chat.

One way to test the waters is to enroll in a foreign language course abroad, such as the one my friend Claudette signed up for: a four-week intensive French immersion course in the picturesque town of Villefranche-sur-Mer, on the French Riviera. After four weeks of French immersion, she moved to Paris. After nine months she moved back to her apartment in the States, but she continues to go back to Paris at least once a year, coming home to work and to gather enough money together so she can get back to France. If you Google "Language Courses Abroad," you will find hundreds of schools scattered across the globe, where you can learn Italian, Spanish, French, German, Greek, and just about any language you could hope to learn. And doesn't it make sense to study a language in the country where that language is spoken? Of course it does. And while you're at it, you can get acclimated to the local wines and cuisine, while taking in the sights. It's a tough, thankless job, but it's got to be done, if you want to get a feel for the country.

If you have the time, the inclination, and the money to try a new country on for size—for, say, three to six months—you might even be able to work out a house trade or two. There are many sites online that deal with house swapping. I have friends who exchange houses on a fairly regular basis, and their comfy but modest house in Los Angeles has snagged them a spacious Montmartre apartment and a house in La Rochelle. Other friends have swapped for houses in Ireland and Spain. Another Los Angeles couple I know swaps houses with a couple in San Francisco, when they want to be in Northern California for yearly family get-togethers. Pick a foreign country, or just go out of state. Chances are there's someone with a house or apartment in another part of the world who is looking for exactly what you've got, even if you don't think where you live might be the most desirable holiday destination. It very well might be for someone.

Swapping houses is a great way to try out another way of life, if you're toying with the idea of becoming an expat; or even if you're toying with the idea of moving to another state, or moving from the city to a rustic country home. Sometimes we have—shall we say—romantic notions of what life must be like in a foreign country. Likewise, if you're a city dweller and have always dreamed of living in a small country town, or a tiny community on a little island, you might want to test it out for a few months. Specifically, a few months off-season, when the population goes from a high of, say, two thousand, back down to the year-round population of eighty-five. Living in a small community has its pros and cons, which should become crystal clear after a few weeks. If you're used to the anonymity that a large city affords you, the magnifying glass of a small town might take some getting used to. Everyone will know your business, sooner or later. Which may sound like a little slice of heaven to you. But if you're not accustomed to that kind of scrutiny, it might be best to give it a test-drive. A friend of mine spent a few weeks on a bucolic island off Washington state, and was rather disconcerted when she noticed the inhabitants waving at her. Waving, every time she drove by. At first she thought she knew the person waving, then she realized that everyone just *waves* at everyone else. If you find that sort of friendliness unnerving, then a small town may be just a little too quaint for you.

In any event, the world is your oyster. It really is! You may be thinking, "Oh, that's all well and good for you, but some of us have to work for a living. I will have to work until I am ninety-five. I don't have a pension, nor do I have a house I can sell to finance such a dream. Go away. I have to get back to work. I can never, ever stop working." Well, you may be thinking that, but you may be creating your own obstacle. Unless you really love your work and you *want* to work your fingers to the bone or punch a clock until you're one-hundred-and-two.

It really is a matter of will. People have always done the craziest things in order to do what they had a mind to do. Blind people have crossed oceans in small sailboats all by themselves, for heaven's sake. Helen Hooven Santmyer spent fifty years writing her novel . . . *And Ladies of the Club*, which was published when she was eighty-eight years old. I am betting that she didn't sit around whining about how she shouldn't bother writing her book because "I'm too old and no one will publish it anyway." Julia Child was well into her thirties before she even learned to cook! Her first cookbook wasn't published until she was almost fifty. Laura Ingalls Wilder didn't publish her first book (*Little House on the Prairie* and the subsequent series) until she was *sixty-five*. Harriet Doerr got her degree from Stanford when she was sixty-seven years old, and went on to publish *Stones for Ibarra*, winning the National Book Award. Apparently our creative juices don't get the whole "I'm too old" concept.

So once you stop setting little mental roadblocks for yourself, you just have to figure out what it is you want to be doing, and where it is you'd like to be doing it. And if "I won't have enough money unless I work forever" is one of your personal roadblocks, you should look into the cost of living in other parts of the world. There are ways to live in other countries on the cheap. Of course, if life is not worth living without five-star hotels, Louboutins, and a new wardrobe every season, then you might not feel comfortable living on a paltry budget. But remember that old fable about the Mexican fisherman and the CEO—the executive had worked his entire life and amassed a great fortune so he could retire in a picturesque fishing village, something the Mexican fisherman had been doing all along. Most people think they need to work a lifetime raking in the dough, just so they can live in a lovely place, take a boat out, catch a few fish, have a nice siesta with the spouse every afternoon, play with the grandkids, and enjoy time with friends and family. Other people opt to live a simple life without the years of toil or the golden parachute. Cut to the chase! Skip the conventional wisdom that says you can't retire until you've got such and such in your IRA. Maybe there's a little fishing village with your name on it, if you're interested in—and willing to—live a simple life.

A **PEARL OF WISDOM** FOR THE CHILD WHO HAS LEFT HOME

Call your mother. Okay? Just call, once in a while. Thanks, hon.

part 4

They're Baaa-aack...

22 Nails on a Chalkboard

When Your Child Comes Home on Holiday

NOW THAT YOU'RE NO LONGER LIVING FULL-TIME WITH YOUR offspring, you might notice certain changes in your relationship with your child. You may find that you get along fine from a distance, but when you get together on college breaks, it's like oil and water.

Well, part of your child's evolution—which started when he became a teenager, in case you missed it—is to separate himself from his family. The process of discovering just how much smarter, wiser, and more evolved he is than his dad and mom began in his early teens, but his newfound freedom and life away from you have added a certain swagger to his bearing. A smugness. An irritating confidence. And simply put, he is annoyed by you, pretty much constantly. It's because he finds you so predictable.

Your children have spent at least eighteen years with you. Is it any wonder they roll their eyes when you do that thing? You know. That . . . *thing* you do. You will be forever pegged as the gal who does *that thing*. They can predict exactly how you'll react to any given situation. They know precisely what will set you off on a rant. They know that when they make a deeply profound comment about something, you will make a pun, and then you'll laugh at your own pun. They are all too familiar with the habit you have of reading billboards aloud as you drive down the street. They are very much acquainted with the way you scream at the umpires on the TV, and leave Post-it notes on the bathroom mirror. They have seen it all. Their familiarity has bred a sublime sense of superiority.

Just go with it. Let them lord it over you. They still love you, albeit in a smug, supercilious way. At some point they will begin to appreciate your puns, your inane chatter, your well-meaning questions about their love life. Not now. Maybe not for quite a while. But be patient. It'll happen. In the meantime, think about all those things that make you so damn predictable. Maybe it's time you got out of a few personality ruts yourself.

Maybe next time you're driving with them, you'll refrain from making comments about the moronic driving habits of every person you're driving behind. Maybe you won't scold them next time you find them playing basketball in the rain, telling them they'll "catch cold." Or "get wet." I mean, they're going to get wet. That's the fun part, duh. Maybe you'll surprise them with a new opinion you've formed, or a change of heart about something you've always been adamantly against, or for. Maybe if you've never had an opinion about anything, they'll be surprised to find out that you do have a few. Or that you're willing to listen to theirs.

And, um, cut them a little slack. You know what I mean? If your little Homecoming Queen who favored polo shirts and pastels comes home for spring break in dreadlocks, smelling of patchouli, and with an irritating penchant for saying "Irie" with a disconcerting grin, just . . . go with it. If your former math nerd comes home for the winter holidays with a new goatee—that he's dyed a bright indigo blue—don't make any snide remarks. Just don't. Even when you notice that his tongue is pierced. It's okay. I mean, ow. But still, don't mention it, especially not with that a smug chuckle of yours. They're experimenting. Out in the big world. Even though it seems as if they're just running with the herd, they're being brave. That's a good thing. They should be commended.

Keep them on their toes, too. Remember, they've only known you for eighteen, nineteen, twenty years. They don't know who you were before you had children. They don't know that you used to drive your old clunker up and down the riverbed, or that you spray painted graffiti on freeway overpasses, or that you backpacked naked in the High Sierra, or that you dyed your hair magenta. They don't know about that love affair you had with the bluegrass fiddle player, or about the time you rode a wild boar, or went camping in the snow, or drove across the country in a VW bug. To them, you are simply Mom or Dad. There is no mystery. They have no idea. And even if you never did anything really interesting before you had children, they don't have to know that. Intimate. Drop mysterious hints. Let them wonder. Stop being so predictable. For your own sake, as well as those creatures you raised and have now let loose on the world.

HOLIDAYS AND VACATIONS:
DO THE RULES STILL APPLY?

What about when young Markus or darling Izzy come home for the holidays? A one- or two-week winter break is one thing, but what if she decides she wants to "just hang" for a few months during the summer? Do you revert back to the rules you all agreed on when she was a teenager? Does Lola have a curfew? Does Wesley's girlfriend get to spend the night? *In the same room?* Do your college-age kids get to drink wine with their dinner? Will they be required to check in and let you know whether they'll be home for dinner? Is your brain exploding yet?

Well, first off: The alcohol thing is really between you, your spouse, your gods, and your conscience—and of course, the police, if anything gets out of control. Since my god happens to be called Bacchus, it's not a personal dilemma. When we've visited friends and relatives in France, the children generally are served a small bit of wine or pear cider with dinner, and I guess you can say we've never been averse to them having a little taste now and again. (Let the outrage begin!) When my son was seventeen and on his own for six weeks in Paris (where the legal drinking age is sixteen), he had an occasional beer. Apparently his frugality won out over any possible alcoholic tendencies, because he actually came home under budget, having decided that it cost too much to get blotto. When he comes home from college for holidays, he'll sometimes have a glass of wine with dinner, if we're having wine with dinner. He doesn't have a driver's license, and he knows not to get into a car with anyone who's been drinking alcohol. Yes, thank you, we are aware that he's not allowed to legally drink alcohol in this country. Shhh! Don't tell! But he seems to be handling it with a certain amount of thoughtful consideration, so far. I can't speak for your children, or your relationship with alcohol, so I'll leave that decision up to you.

Of course, the same must go for whether your kids are allowed to have girlfriends or boyfriends spend the night, whether they will have a curfew when they come home, and whether they need to check in every evening they spend out. I mean, you're the parents, right? So maybe you want to think about these questions before the holidays. Think about what your comfort level might be in any of the above situations. For instance, if the walls are thin, or your bedroom wall shares a wall with your son or daughter's room, a thoughtful chat about beds bumping in the night could be in order, if a girlfriend or boyfriend intends to have a sleepover. A sleepover might be too much to allow at this juncture, but you know your kids better than I, so you'll have to make the call.

But here's a thought: Let's say you have a friend visiting from out of town. Let's say your friend isn't just coming to visit you; your friend is in town on business. Your friend is very happy to be staying in your house, and you'll be spending some time together, but your friend also has some other stuff to do. So you won't be hanging out with each other for the entire visit. In this situation, you'd probably want to know which nights your friend intends to have dinner with you. If your friend was breezing in and out of the house and coming and going as she pleased, you might want to know if she was going to be out all night, or whether she'd be back for dinner and that sort of thing. You just don't want to feel as if you're running a motel.

Now, we all have friends who, when they come to visit, we wish would treat our house more like a motel. We just don't want to see them every minute of the day, and we wish they wouldn't hang around so much. So really, this is a personal call, and everything depends upon the kind of freedom your children had when they were living at home. Perhaps they'll have a little more, now that they are no longer children, but that must be your decision. It's your house, and now a young adult is visiting your house. We hope there's still a bed for him, and we trust he won't be too shocked by the giant walk-in closet or crafts room that his old bedroom has become.

RETURN OF THE PRODIGALS

Whether they're home for a short school holiday or for an entire summer, there is one thing you must do to really enjoy the returning child, to really get the most out of having your youngster back in the nest: Completely divest yourself of all expectations. Or at least lower them a little. Because if you don't, every time your young student visits home, every time you attend a Freshman Parents' Visit, every family vacation you take together, you will be disappointed. This is just good advice for life in general; be optimistic, of course. But don't pin every hope and dream on your children, and this especially extends to those small vacations and short visits home.

Your young adults have been away for most of the year, learning new ideas, gaining new insight, finding out who they are outside of the family unit. Don't expect that they're going to want to spend every minute with Mom and Dad when they come home for their first winter break. Don't assume they'll want to sit around the family dinner table expounding on newfound philosophies and discussing their future plans. That kind of thing may not happen for a few years yet. Just because they're in some bastion of higher learning doesn't mean they've instantly matured. Many of them are still scatterbrained teenagers. Many of them did not apply for a summer internship before spring break started, thereby assuring them something to do over their summer break. Many of them will come home, open the fridge, stare in it for too long, then disappear into their old rooms, from which will soon emanate the mellifluous tones of a bootlegged indie hit blasting at a high ten.

Enjoy the moments you have with them. Don't be a doormat to their every whim, and certainly don't allow them to take you for granted. But if you have no expecta-tions, then whatever time you have with them will be gravy.

What Is This "Empty Nest" of Which You Speak?

SOME NESTS DON'T STAY EMPTY. SOME OF YOU ARE PROBABLY looking over at your twenty-two-year-old son sitting on the sofa eating Cheetos, or watching as your twenty-four-year-old daughter grabs her bag and heads out the door for a date, and you're thinking, "Empty nest? What the hell is she talking about?" And here I am going on and on about "empty nest" this, and "quiet house" that, and not even thinking that perhaps you only had a short fling with the empty-nest feeling, the unmistakable sound of nobody home. Sorry! You only had a tiny taste of freedom. Wasn't that yummy? And now the kids are back.

I know, rents are high; the cost of living has skyrocketed. It's tough for a young person to extricate himself from the comfort of the home fires. Maybe your child graduated from high school and has been living at home while attending a local college; perhaps he went to work directly out of high school. Maybe he came home after his college graduation, "just for a couple of months" while he got on his feet. And now you've all settled into a comfortable arrangement that doesn't appear to have an end in sight.

But are you making it a little *too* comfortable? I know he's no longer a child, and you may have qualms about setting house rules, but if your children get to use your house as a free crash pad, why would they ever leave? If you've got a strapping twentysomething inhaling snacks at 1 a.m., hogging the TV to watch reruns of *Family Guy* at odd hours of the day, and allowing you to do his laundry, then it could be years before you again experience the joy of the empty nest.

I do know that it's not always easy—or affordable—for your child to spread his wings. And it's perfectly understandable that you'd be more than happy to welcome your son or daughter back home, just to help out while they sort out employment and living situations. You may have a particularly close relationship with your son or daughter—and if you both enjoy each other's company and you cohabitate peacefully, then inviting your child back for a stretch might suit you both just fine.

But time has a way of passing, the days and months go by, and all of a sudden it's "Hello, *Grey Gardens*." Before you know it you're both eating cat food on toast points and walking around in bras and sun hats, talking to feral cats and thinking that everything is perfectly normal, and it's everyone *else* who's got the problem.

But there are ways to gently nudge your freeloader—I mean, adored offspring—out of that comfy nest. For instance, you could calculate how much rent your child would have to pay if he was out in the big world having to pay for his own place. If you've decided, in sound mind, to let your children move back in with you, take advantage of the situation. If they can't afford to pay you rent, put them to work for their room and board. Basic chores are a given: They should be eagerly taking out the trash and recycling, as well as sweeping, cleaning up after themselves, and generally neatening up any room they've passed through. But they should also have a regular roster of duties that will help them offset their free rent.

They could start a vegetable garden, and engage in some regular weeding and trimming. And how about finally having a certain someone dig a hole and install that little pond you've been dreaming about? There are lawns to be mowed, rugs to be vacuumed, windows to be washed. I bet your child is clever enough to figure out how to prep and paint a room, refinish a mantelpiece, organize some kitchen cabinets, and scrub the kitchen floors. These are all skills that will be useful to your child when he eventually flees the roost. Which he may do sooner rather than later, if he finds the workload somewhat oppressive. In the meantime, put those kids to work!

Perhaps there should be a limit on how many pajama days in a row are allowed during any given week. If you came home and found your spouse in his or her pajamas in the afternoon, day after day, watching TV and playing computer games, you might assume that your spouse was suffering from some sort of depression. If your child isn't already depressed, she soon will be, if only from lack of sunshine and exercise. Everyone needs a pajama day from time to time. But if you ate ice cream for breakfast every morning, it would no longer be a special treat, right?

Groceries should also be a part of the equation. If they eat their meals at home, they ought to help out with the grocery shopping and cooking, if they're not able to contribute to the cost. Is it really too much to ask that they cook dinner at least once a week, or be able to follow a basic grocery list?

This is all supposing that your kids haven't yet found work, or otherwise gotten on their feet. If they *have* found employment but you want to help them out so they're not spending three-quarters of their paycheck on rent, that's very nice of you, and I hope they're showing you gobs of appreciation. In some cases, it really does make sense to combine forces to create some kind of temporary communal-living situation. But even if your adult child is working full-time, it doesn't mean you should become his full-time servant. He still needs to behave as if he's an actual non-feral human being, and help around the house. Just as he'd be expected to do if he lived with a bunch of roommates.

If your house has become little more than a way station for your youngsters—albeit one requiring constant maintenance—why not put your house to work for you? Have your live-in children act as caretakers while you hop a tramp steamer and take an extended trip to the South Seas, or go live on a barge on the French canals for a year, as I plan to do. Your "caretakers" can advertise for a few roommates who will rent your extra rooms at market value, and your offspring will be responsible for keeping the house explosion-free while you're gone. After months of traveling the globe, you'll be ready to return to your cozy house, and your child will probably be more than ready to find an apartment of his own.

There is something to be said for intergenerational living, and outside of our western culture extended families live together as a matter of course. In Japan, Africa, India, and the Middle East, elderly parents are traditionally revered, and it's understood that their children will care for them as they age.

One big happy family living together under one roof. Children, grandchildren, moms and dads, grandparents, all taking care of one another. It sounds idyllic, and certainly if you can make it work with your own family, I applaud you. Your kids will save a bundle living under the family roof, and when they get married, they can move in their husbands and wives. I'm sure your daughter-in-law will adore you. Their children will benefit from living with loving grandparents, aunts, and uncles, and the grandparents will benefit from the extra hands around the house. Everyone will benefit from the companionship. That is, if everyone commits to real communal living, pulling their weight and doing their fair share.

So sure, the kids can move back in, as long as they don't treat the family commune like a hotel, and you don't end up being expected to provide maid and room service. It could be a nice way to live, and I really wouldn't mind at all. As long as I can come and go as I please and am not expected to cook for nineteen people every night. Or make beds. Or do other people's dishes all the time. And as long as I have a room I can call my own and can be alone in the house once in a while. And a little quiet, please. Is that too much to ask?

EMPTY NESTUS INTERRUPTUS

So, your kid is in college. Great! He even got into a really good university where he's studying something complicated that may actually enable him to have a career. He lives in the dorms, and has a really nice roommate. He enjoys the dining hall, and occasional campus activities. But not on the weekends. Because the thing is, this wonderful citadel of higher learning, this bustling campus full of eager, curious youngsters happens to be only a few short miles from where you live. Just the way it worked out. And now here you are, discovering the joys of the empty nest—but only on the weekdays. When the weekend comes around, there's your beaming boy or darling daughter, ready for a home-cooked meal and looking forward to a couple of days of sleeping in and lounging around in the ol' pj's. While you do the laundry.

You may enjoy having him home for a weekend or two, but at the same time, your child is neither here nor there; one foot in college life, the other foot still firmly planted in his childhood bedroom. He never gets to really know his classmates outside of class, because he is going to his classes and doing schoolwork all week long. On Friday, he hightails it home, missing out on weekend hikes and weekend parties and weekend concerts with people he sees every day in school, and could be getting to know better.

You could be wondering about your own life, "What if the weekend was like the rest of the week, full of . . . no children? Hm, I wonder." Maybe it's time to encourage your young commuter to try a few weekends on campus. If you are saving money by not paying for the student meal plan during the weekend, well, think about how much you're really saving. Maybe you could drop off some sandwich fixings, a bag of fruit, a loaf of bread, and a jar of peanut butter to his dorm room, as an experiment. Give him a few bucks to get dinner at the dining hall. Encourage him to start joining in more campus activities on the weekends. Exhort him to put both feet in, to see what it's like to be a full-time student. He can come home anytime, but as long as he's "away" at college, he might as well commit.

A **PEARL OF WISDOM** FOR THE CHILD WHO HAS LEFT HOME

Pretend you already are who and what you want to be.

YOUR CHILD, OUT IN THAT BIG, BAD WORLD

Sometimes children literally flee their childhood homes in their eagerness to get out from under the family thumb, but some have a harder time disconnecting themselves from home and hearth. But maybe your child is reluctant to fly the coop because she senses that you've been reluctant to let her go.

It's lovely that you have always had such a close relationship, it really is. But perhaps you inadvertently sent your child a few mixed messages while she was growing up; she may have gotten the message that the world is a dark, scary place, full of threats to her safety and well-being. She could have been snatched off the street at any moment; buses and subways are full of crazy and violent people; even walking on a city street is just asking for trouble. She might have ventured to the mall a few times in high school, with a group of friends, if she had a ride. But she never really had an interest in learning how to navigate a city, or travel by bus or subway, or walk anywhere by herself.

But this is exactly why it's a good idea to encourage her to go off to college—or perhaps study abroad for a year—these rites of passage are a great way to jump in the deep end of the pool. If she opted for a local city college and she's still hanging about the house far too much, see if she might be open to the idea of exploring the larger world and possibly a larger campus in her sophomore year. Take a trip to a bigger city together, if you're both used to a more suburban way of life. Field trip! Walk on the streets, take a subway, have an adventure. You can be cautious without being fearful, which will show your almost-adult child how to embrace the world in a positive way. (And there are plenty of small colleges in rural settings, if that might make her feel better about being on her own.)

24

You, Your Roommates, and the Rules

I KNOW, YOU'VE MISSED THEM TERRIBLY. YOU THINK IT WOULD be fantastic to have them home again, now that they're more grown-up. But you should know that when your grown children come back to live with you, they might just revert back to their teen-age selves. It's just the way it seems to work in families, at least most of the time. So you really will have to set some ground rules, if you want to be master of your domain.

Setting rules are one thing; enforcing them is quite another. You may believe that your grown children should be doing their own laundry, for instance. But if you have the kind of youngster who has rarely lifted a finger around the house, he may see no reason why he should start now. And he will do everything to avoid it. He will attempt to outlast you. And he probably will. He'll think, "Dad or Mom will eventually be doing their own laundry, I will just throw my clothes in with theirs. It's a win-win! For me, anyway." He will go out and buy new underwear to avoid having to do his laundry.

He will sleep in the same sheets for months at a time. When you see his pants standing up by themselves in the corner of his room, you may start to waver. When his pants tip over and attempt to crawl to the washing machine by themselves, you will be doubly tempted to break down and do his laundry. Don't do it!

Not to turn your life into a series of petty "that's not my job" bickerings. But a balance has to be struck. If you have decided that it's too much to ask your adult child to work for his room and board, at least make a deal. You will do all the laundry if he agrees to clean the bathroom and empty the dishwasher. Or something along those lines. Make a "chore chart" and put it on the refrigerator, just like you did when he was in elementary school. If they're going to behave like children, they might have to be treated like children.

Try to actually enforce a few ground rules. If you had grown-up roommates, you'd expect a few basics, so you shouldn't expect less from your grown children. As grown-up as your children become, you don't ever stop being a parent. Of course you want to help smooth the rough spots, and you want to give them a hand when you can—whether they are living five hundred miles away or are still sharing your refrigerator. But the same thing applies whether they're six or twenty-six; you're doing them no favors by doing everything for them.

25

You, the Model of Gracious Living

OKAY, SO LET'S SAY YOUR KIDS HAVE BEEN TO COLLEGE AND HAVE come back after graduation, or they're taking some college courses while still living at home, or one of them got a local job after high school and it just seems impractical for him to spend most of his paycheck on rent. In any event, the kids haven't ventured too far from the nest. Could this be because you have always encouraged and welcomed them to live "at home"?

I'm not suggesting that you boot your little darlings out of the nest the day after their eighteenth birthday. But I am suggesting that some kids are a little less motivated than others to spread their wings. So if you decide to let your semi-grown-up children live with you for an indeterminate amount of time, possibly forever, in some kind of nebulous, undefined arrangement, be warned: You will likely be doing as much parenting as you did when they were teenagers. You may think you're not, but you'll still be fretting over your parenting, or worrying that perhaps you've been neglectful, or wondering if you've done too much, or are not doing enough.

Just because your kids are now "adults" doesn't mean they will act like adults. Not when they are used to being children in your house. Meanwhile, they're still taking their cues from you, whether consciously or not. Your way of life is now the model for your children. Sure, they're adults, or on the cusp of adulthood. But in some ways, they're still as impressionable as five-year-olds. The way you live, eat, behave, accept challenges, and rise to any occasion will be indelibly imprinted on their psyches. If you allow them to come back and live with you, you will be their model for adult living, whether you mean to be or not. Here is your chance to show them how grown-ups live.

Okay, so let's say your house is a little bit of a mess—dishes piled up in the sink, tables cluttered with papers, more dishes, someone's computer, bills, coffee cups. When your kids were young, you had an excuse. Or at least more of an excuse. But not so much anymore. And now your kids are getting used to the clutter and the chaos. You are modeling a chaotic way of life to your children. They think this is how grown-ups live. Is this the message you want to send to them?

If they are, how shall I say . . . couch potatoes? And they have become aware over the years, that you, too, prefer the comfort of the sofa, the television, and a jumbo-size bag of Doritos, then, well, who can blame them for following in Mom or Dad's footsteps? Conversely, if they've become couch potatoes and they see you being very active, then it will become very clear to them that they are being kind of couch potato-y. Every time you take off for a game of paddle tennis or go on a hike in the canyon, they will become more aware how little they're doing. They will notice the contrast. And maybe they'll want to do something about it. Telling them they are lazy couch potatoes really doesn't do a bit of good, if you remember how well that used to go over in the teenage years. But seeing you— an elderly, decrepit parent—running out the door and bounding around the house in a decidedly *un*-decrepit manner, well, maybe the television will eventually lose some of its appeal.

The same goes for the way you deal with conflict. If you are quick to anger and explode at the slightest provocation; if you fall apart at the slightest bit of adversity, just remember that the young people in your house are still learning from you how people handle the rough patches. And honestly, isn't life just a bit too short to spend it screaming at glitchy appliances and people who make mistakes?

There are upsides to being models for your offspring. For instance, if you are struggling on a limited budget, but are doing your best to get by, they'll see how you do that, too. When they see you making lemonade from a giant vat of lemons, they'll know that it's possible to turn adversity around. If they see you handle challenges with aplomb and watch you laugh in the face of disaster, that'll rub off on them too. It's relatively easy to learn how to clean a bathroom; you can always teach them how to do that. But if your kids learn from you how to gracefully navigate life's bumpy road, it will be the most valuable lesson you can teach them, and will serve them well for years to come.

HEY, THANKS!

So you'll go through ups and downs after the kids move on. But come on, whether you had kids or not you'd be going through ups and downs, right? There is no reason why the downs have to dominate. Everything you've gone through has led you to where you are right now. If you're dwelling on your "failures," just imagine if you hadn't gone through those experiences. You might never have traveled to a certain place, you might never have had children, or ended up taking that part-time job.

"But I hated that job!" you say. Yes, I know! But if you'd never taken that job, you would never have stumbled into that bookstore on that certain day, where you met that person, or read that book, or experienced that event that changed your life. If you find yourself whining a little too long and hard about the same thing year after year; if you find yourself saying things like, "Why does this keep happening to me?" then maybe it's time to change the channel. You've done so many remarkable things. You have had such a fine life. And now you get to have more of it! You can look at a black-and-white photograph and focus only on the dark part, or you can look at the whole picture, and see how all the parts fit together to make an interesting image.

You don't have to be that person anymore, you really don't. You don't have to be the person who always has to point out the downside. You don't have to be the guy who points out how something might not go well, before you even do it. You don't have to be the one whose life is not exactly what you thought it would be, while everyone else seems to be getting exactly what they want.

Try waking up every morning and being truly grateful, down to your bones, for all that you have. This does not require a belief in God, or a god, or many gods. It can simply be a general "Hey, thanks!" like you mean it. Because, look at you! Take it in for a minute. Kids are launched. You've got the rest of your wonderful life ahead of you. And how exciting is that?

A **PEARL OF WISDOM** FOR THE CHILD WHO HAS LEFT HOME

Get some exercise! I'm talking to you, sweetie. Get up and move that body around! Start making a habit of exercising now, and you'll be so happy when you're older.

YOUR SHIFTING RELATIONSHIP

If your kids have been off enjoying their first year of college, when you do see them, you'll suddenly be aware of the limited time you have with them. You'll find you want to make the most of that time. Those moments happen less often than they used to, and they will probably happen a lot less from here on out. You probably are going to want your time together to be the best it can be. The moments you share with your kids are so few and far between, you will do things like listen to a radio station you hate while you're driving somewhere with him, because your kid happens to love that station. Yes, you will sit through mind-numbing electronic pop and inane lyrics for an entire twenty-minute car ride. You'll take him out for a hamburger, even though you're trying to watch your weight and you don't really eat hamburgers anymore. You'll want to go shopping with her even if you hate shopping. You just want to make every day a holiday.

Eventually you'll be developing an entirely different relationship with your adult child, one that might be difficult to make a transition into, at first. Try not to put them in the same boxes they were in when they were five or ten years old. Just because Max "was never very good with his hands!" doesn't mean that Max is going to be a klutz for the rest of his life. Assume that your children will evolve into new people, and that different facets of their personalities might mature and ripen. I'm sure you hated going home as a twenty- or thirtysomething, and being known as the "Funny One," or the "Sensitive One," or the "Sullen One." It's hard enough going back to the family home and not falling into our old roles. Why do kids want to move away from home? So they can reinvent themselves, just like we wanted to do when we moved out on our own. Help your children out by not pigeonholing them. Keep your ears open. Rediscover who they are and be open to who they are striving to be.

The Really, Really Empty Nest

When Your Child Gets Married

SO, YOU THOUGHT IT WAS ROUGH WHEN YOUR CHILD WENT OFF to college? Now your daughter tells you she's getting married and moving to another state. Your son has moved in with his longtime girlfriend and they're planning on tying the knot this summer. You are about to be just another in-law.

You used to be able to count on your kids coming home for spring break and Christmas. But this marriage and/or partnership has caused them to inexplicably want their *own* lives and their own holidays. Away from their mother and father, who love them. Why, oh why?

Well, as they used to say, you're not losing a son or daughter, you're gaining a daughter- or son-in-law. And really, if you haven't yet gotten over your young man or woman moving away from home and into the dorms, it's time to snip that last bit of umbilical cord. Do your best to establish a good relationship with your new daughter- or son-in-law, no matter what you may think of that person now. If you sense the partner your son or daughter has chosen is like oil to your water, don't rush to judgment. Be the sensible rock of wisdom and venerability. Perhaps "Kill Them with Kindness" sends the wrong message, but you get the idea.

Welcome the new spouse or partner into the family, but avoid being overbearing. Your grown children—with or without their new partners—shouldn't be required to come for Sunday dinner just because you've always made Sunday dinner for the family, and Sunday is Family Night. Maybe your kids want to start their own Family Nights, and make their own Sunday dinners. Maybe they'll even invite you, once in a while. Family traditions are wonderful and to be cherished, but we can go overboard. Traditions should never be forced; let them happen organically. If you make your own delicious and inviting Sunday dinner, it might just happen to turn into a tradition with friends and family because everyone loves coming to your house to eat and see one another. But as soon as it becomes an obligation, uh-oh. Don't make your kids feel as if they're expected to come every single week. If you want to slave all day over a brisket, do it because you love making Sunday dinner, not because The Family Always Eats Together on Sunday Night. Ugh. There's no need to seethe over the pot roast as one more Sunday goes by with your adult children making excuses for not being able to come for dinner. Either figure out a way to enjoy your time alone, or think about widening your circle of acquaintances. Because, remember? You're a self-assured and independent person, whose happiness is not dependent upon the whims of anyone, especially your children.

The same goes for holidays. As your children grow up and start living their own lives, they may not want to spend every Thanksgiving, Christmas, and New Year's Eve with you. Buck up. You could look at this as more time to spread your wings, too. And pat yourself

on the back for a job well done; isn't it nice to know your children have been successfully launched into their own lives and are enjoying their own families? Yes it is.

And excuse me, but a *wedding*? How fun would that be? Very, is what. There are worse things than a wedding, right? Food, dancing, getting all dressed up, weeping as the happy couple strides up the aisle (or walks barefoot through the organic vegetable garden, depending what kind of kids you've got). You can offer organizational or monetary help, but if the youngsters want to put on their own show, then eat, dance, and enjoy simply being an honored guest.

And if any of your children suddenly start having their own children, well, again—don't turn it into an opportunity to be the boss of the backyard. Instead, be the Serene High Grandparent of Insight, Helpfulness, and Infectious Fun. Think *Auntie Mame* rather than Aunt March. Offer your infinite wisdom sparingly, or when asked. Give generously of blankets, binkies, and books; and your time, if you can. Offer as much help as you can to the new parents, but know when to butt out.

A **PEARL OF WISDOM** FOR THE CHILD WHO HAS LEFT HOME

Remember, you can always call your mom. And your dad, too. But seriously. You can always call your mom. Like, right now might be a good time.

Parenting: The Final Frontier

OKAY, HERE'S ME, CRACKING THE WHIP. ARE YOU OVER IT YET? Your last offspring has traipsed off to college, or taken off to the Far East with a train pass in his knapsack, or moved in with a bunch of friends. You're all torn up. I get it. But do you not yet understand how much fun this will be? How much fun you could be having *right this minute*? Have we not talked about fun enough? You've got the world on a string, as they say. This is not a chore. This is not some horrible trial that you must endure. Seriously, if you're still moping about, wondering why your children aren't falling all over themselves to write you daily letters, send you constant e-mails, and call you every night before bed, then you just aren't hearing me. This is *fun*, people. You get the house to yourself. And it just got a whole lot bigger. Your time is your own. Oh, boohoo, how will I ever fill the void of my empty days, now that I am no longer needed to make snacks and be an on-call chauffeur?! Seriously?

I understand it's a bit of a blow. Especially if your only child just left, and you don't have any "backup" children. I mean, yeah, that's rough, if the only child you have never calls you. You can't console yourself with the thought that your eldest always calls on Sunday, so it's okay if the youngest hasn't called you since Mother's Day last year, a day late. But you see, this is what I'm talking about; it was true in high school—when the sun rose and set on some indifferent boy—and it's truer now than it's ever been. It is never a good idea for your happiness to depend entirely on another person. We can love our loved ones, we can cherish them, we can enjoy the love we get back from them, but it's not their job to make us happy. It's not their job to complete us. They didn't sign up for that job, and it's not really fair for you to give them that job. Especially if you signed them up for that job without them knowing. You mustn't let them volunteer for that job, either, just because they have good hearts. Because, you know, that's kind of an impossible job.

It's also a burden that no one should have to bear, someone else's happiness. It's a lot of responsibility. And right now, your kids are taking on a whole lot of other responsibilities. You don't want them to be going through life secretly cringing at your neediness, do you? I bet you'd hate being thought of as clingy. My friend Wendy has the perfect word for it: glommy. Please don't be glommy. It just doesn't suit you. It's not really attractive on anyone. I'm sure you would frown upon your son or daughter becoming deeply involved with a person who was so dependent upon them that their every mood was affected by how much attention they were getting. Who needs the drama?

And I don't mean "living your own life" as in a sniffy, "I'm going to live my own life all right, I'll never call them ever again and then they'll be sorry!" kind of way. Show your children that being independent, self-sufficient, and self-assured gives you a sturdy foundation for healthy relationships. Including the one between you and them.

Remember how you felt about your parents when you were in your twenties? I imagine most of you didn't really see the point of having parents when you were that age. Your parents were just those people who lived in the house where you grew up, where you liked to crash from time to time; where you could count on a good home-cooked meal and maybe spend your holidays. Or sometimes they were those people you moved as far away from as possible. You put thousands of miles between you for one reason or another. Parents were parents. You put up with them in a patronizing way, when you thought of them at all.

But maybe as you got older, you eventually realized that your parents had a limited shelf life. Perhaps you gravitated back to them, knowing that they wouldn't be around forever. Maybe you ended up having a pretty close relationship with them, as you realized how much you inexplicably had in common. You finally came to appreciate that putting up with their idiosyncrasies and annoying personality traits was simply a part of growing up. In fact, you may have even embraced their annoying personality traits, recognizing that you both might be cut from the same cloth.

So just trust that your kids will eventually gravitate back to you, especially if you let them break away, as they're supposed to be doing at their age. Eventually they'll come to embrace your annoying personality traits, too.

I leave you with this empty-nest checklist for easy reference:

Don't wallow in your Empty-Nestness. Do not indulge in a sad Empty-Nest-a-thon. You've created the perfect child. Now go create your perfect life.

Keep Post-it notes around to write down your own Pearls of Wisdom for the Child Who Has Left Home (see page 35). Make sure you write down "Call Mom!" on a handful of them.

Remind yourself, from time to time, that you can dance in the living room wearing nothing but a vintage apron and a pair of gym socks. Anytime you want.

Relish the daydreaming, plotting, planning, imagining, and fantasizing about the child-free life you have stretched out in front of you.

Enjoy the time you do have with your kids. Lowering your expectations doesn't have to be a negative thing.

It's not too late to _____! (Fill in the blank. It pretty much works for everything. Except time travel, or becoming a Russian cosmonaut.)

Learning doesn't stop just because you no longer help your kids with their homework.

Discover your own backyard. Then discover what's over the fence.

Eat, drink, and be merry with your friends, as often as possible.

Embrace your evolving beauty, and continue to cultivate your sense of humor, because you will need it most of all.

Redecorate or run away from home . . . think about where you want to be next week, and five years from now.

It's not just about filling your time with as many activities as possible, it's about what kind of person you are when you're doing those activities.

Also: Dare to do nothing.

Cut yourself some slack. Cut your kids some slack. Enjoy every bit of time you have together. Because, you know, life is too short, and all that.

Life is grand!

There are worse things than the kids moving back in.

Now go enjoy your newly minted empty nest, and the rest of your child-free years. Not that you ever want to be entirely free of your children. But still. You've earned a nice break from the parenting trenches. Use it well!

ACKNOWLEDGMENTS

I'D LIKE TO ACKNOWLEDGE my enthusiastic and helpful editor, Jodi Warshaw; Christine Carswell, Lisa Tauber, and all the nice people at Chronicle Books who helped to make the book look so good; and the ever-wonderful Jack Jensen: Chronicle Books people are the best. Thanks to Edison Mellor-Goldman for tips and inspiration, and to all the good children who have left home, allowing us parents to enjoy our delightfully empty nests! But do come home soon for a visit.